The Key

by Linda Velez

DORRANCE PUBLISHING CO
EST. 1920
PITTSBURGH, PENNSYLVANIA 15238

The contents of this work, including, but not limited to, the accuracy of events, people, and places depicted; opinions expressed; permission to use previously published materials included; and any advice given or actions advocated are solely the responsibility of the author, who assumes all liability for said work and indemnifies the publisher against any claims stemming from publication of the work.

All Rights Reserved
Copyright © 2021 by Linda Velez

No part of this book may be reproduced or transmitted, downloaded, distributed, reverse engineered, or stored in or introduced into any information storage and retrieval system, in any form or by any means, including photocopying and recording, whether electronic or mechanical, now known or hereinafter invented without permission in writing from the publisher.

Dorrance Publishing Co
585 Alpha Drive
Pittsburgh, PA 15238
Visit our website at *www.dorrancebookstore.com*

ISBN: 978-1-6491-3180-5
EISBN: 978-1-6491-3699-2

For Nana
Thanks for all the help
From both sides of the veil

Forward

This book is not about me. Not an autobiography. It is, rather, about my personal spiritual and psychic story, which includes my decades of study and subsequent growth, which led me to the point that I was able to receive The Key when I had the development to do so.

This book is also about You, Dear Reader, and what The Key and its message mean to you personally.

This book is also about God, from whom I received The Key for You at my request.

May its message bring you love, peace, enlightenment, and eternal joy.

Contents

Forward v

Part 1 – ME 1
    Chapter 1: The Early Years 3
    Chapter 2: Off to School 7
    Chapter 3: Teen Years 13
    Chapter 4: 2nd Decade 23
    Chapter 5: 3rd Decade 29
    Chapter 6: 4th Decade 37
    Chapter 7: 5th Decade 45
    Chapter 8: 6th Decade 51
    Chapter 9: A Visionary?! 55

Part 2 – YOU 61
    Chapter 10: Welcome to Yourself 63
    Chapter 11: Heaven and Beyond 73
    Chapter 12: The Negative Side 81

Part 3 – GOD 95
    Chapter 13: What God Is Not 97
    Chapter 14: What God Is 99

Books/Bibliography 101
Recommended People/Places/Sources/Things of Interest 107

Part 1
ME

Chapter 1

The Early Years

The Key is a symbolic graphic design given to me in a mystical vision not for myself, but for all Humanity at my request. It is for our mass understanding.

To properly tell of how The Key came to be, it is imperative that I tell you the story of my life's journey from a progressive energy angle, which shows the slow and ever-increasing evolution of my spiritual understanding and senses.

I was born in Ossining, New York, U.S.A., on April 23, 1951, in the Ossining Hospital. I was brought home a week later to our 1865 Queen Anne style Victorian home which was on a dead-end street. The street ran along the crest of a hill, which had a millionaire's view of the Hudson River Valley to the west. From our large L-shaped front porch, my brothers and I played, ate, and peered through binoculars at the river with all the boats and ships and the Hudson Highlands beyond. We had a perfect view of Croton Point and Haverstraw at the far side. We watched the town grow and spread out over the years. The view inspired me to draw and paint many pictures of that view's ever-changing colors and moods.

The street was lined, for the most part, with grand old houses from the Victorian era, and in its heyday it was a well to do neighborhood. By the time my family had bought the house in the late 1940s it had become a racially mixed middle class neighborhood. All our neighbors were good, steady, hardworking people. A local minister and his family from the Star of Bethlehem Baptist Church lived on our street. Our doors were never locked. All the kids on the street played together and got along. In my youthful innocence, I thought everyone all lived together in mixed neighborhoods and everyone always got along. However, going to school quickly taught me I was mistaken in my innocent assumption.

Our house was haunted. At night I would see orbs and streaks of light in the darkness in my room and the hallway outside. There was an entity in my closet that was harmless, but I would never open it at night because it scared me. There were little sounds and tapping noises all around at night. Nobody spoke of it, like it was not happening. It scared me, but I kept quiet about the subject because no one else talked about it.

My family consisted of myself, my brothers, (one younger, two older), my parents, and my mother's parents, Nana and Pop. While growing up it seemed I had two mothers and two fathers. I never knew my dad's parents, as they were both deceased by the time I was born. I remember as a young child how surprised I was to learn that most everyone actually has two grandmothers and two grandfathers! We attended the local First Presbyterian Church. My brothers and I attended Sunday school there. The adults in our family rarely attended church.

My earliest memory was being in the backyard of our house on a very hot summer day. I was in the yard watching my older brothers playing in a large galvanized metal washtub as if it were a kiddy pool. Our mom was standing nearby. There were men busily installing aluminum siding to the outside of our house.

Suddenly, Nana came out the back porch carrying a tray of freshly made ice cold lemonade. She called the men down for a cold drink. They climbed down quickly and, wiping away their sweat, gratefully took the glasses. I clearly remembered one of the men wiping away his sweat and saying, "Gee thanks, lady, that sure is good and cold!" He appeared to be beaming as he said this, as his gratitude was so great.

My next earliest memory was being stuck in a playpen. I hated it and wanted out of jail! I was standing up holding onto the bars and yelling at the top of my lungs that I wanted out, but I could not speak yet, so it just came out as baby babble. I clearly remember being hopping mad. Mom told me years later that I learned that if I jumped up and down enough on the floor of my "jail" that it would fall out and I could crawl out from underneath to freedom and mayhem. I guess my stubborn, never-give-up attitude was in-born as well as my being psychic and empathic.

I was also born clairvoyant. One day, when I was about three, I asked my grandmother, "Nana, why us it when people are in a bad mood they have dark clouds rolling around over their heads?"

She showed immediate understanding by nodding her head and letting out a long slow, "Ahh." Then she said, "That's because you're like me. We're different from most people. We can see and hear things most other people can't. We're special, but we can't tell other people about it, because they will not understand. And they will believe there is something wrong with you. They might think you are crazy, even put you away! So don't tell anyone, not Mommy or Daddy, or Pop or your brothers, or anyone else, just me."

Then I told her about the lights I saw and the sounds I heard, and she said, "Oh, those are just 'little reminders' of the people who used to live here, and they can't hurt you."

From that moment on, Nana and I shared a special bond and a closeness that has never abated, even after her death.

Every now and then, she would get an inner prompting and give me advice on the metaphysical. One particular lesson she gave me was that if an entity bothered me that I was to ask it, "What in God's name do you want?" She explained to me that since God is the most powerful, then when you invoke God, it *must* tell you. It cannot resist.

She then told me that I could send an entity away be calling in God again by charging it with, "In the Name of God, be gone!" She explained that it was most important that I *believe* that I can accomplish this, otherwise, it is wasted effort and I could open myself to a terrible attack.

She explained to me that I had a duty of staying in a positive frame of mind and not to fall into the trap of bad/negative thoughts or actions. I had to stay good with God as, if I did not, I would lose my connection to God and I would be open to defeat on a soulic level. There was never any doom and gloom/heaven or hell/sin talk. I believe deep down inside, my grandmother would agree with Mahatma Gandhi that, "God has no religion."

I always believed everything she always told me, and I was never afraid of ghosts or anything else due to her teachings.

There is an unusual occurrence that I have experienced from time to time in this life where I literally see myself through the eyes of another person. My first experience was when I was very young and riding in a stroller being pushed by my mom. I looked down the street at a man who turned his head toward me, and our eyes met. Instantaneously, I was in the man's head. I saw myself in the stroller being pushed along by mom! A second later, I was back into my own self, looking at the man again. He gave me no indication that he had experienced anything at all. I said nothing to my mother of this, just kept it inside. Since then, I have experienced this every now and then, perhaps a dozen times in my life. All were strangers, so I never asked them if they were aware of what happened. Finally, I had the experience with my best friend, so I told her about it. She had noticed nothing herself so that meant I was the one who was "flipping" into other people's minds.

In the present a few years ago, I attended a class given by Kevin Todeshi, CEO of The Association for Research and Enlightenment. The A.R.E. is doing the good work started by Edgar Cayce, known as The Sleeping Prophet. He was America's greatest psychic. I took the opportunity to tell Mr. Todeshi of my flipping experiences and he explained to me that on a deep soulic level I have been experiencing oneness with other people naturally. That was exceedingly interesting to me because most of my life I have been trying to understand the concept of Oneness and wanting to experience it. All the answers *are* inside of us, apparently.

Once a week, my elder brothers and I took a walk to the public library. I always looked forward to it and it has instilled in me a life-long love of books and learning. The library building was a large grand concrete Victorian building that bespoke of an edifice of learning. The front door opened to a small lobby and another door, beyond which, opened to the library itself. I was immediately struck by a colossal open space that was lined with books of untold number. Rows upon rows of freestanding shelves filled with thousands more. The accumulated knowledge of all mankind! If I dared open my mouth, I was immediately hushed up with, "Be quiet! No talking!!"

We then had to walk across the room to a small stairway, which led to the children's library downstairs, which was a fraction of the size and far less grand. Many times I would pause at the top of the stairs and look out over the multitude of books and the people studying at the long rows of tables and I can remember thinking to myself, *When I grow up, I want to read all these books and know* everything! That feeling has never left me, and I learned and retained…

Chapter 2
Off to School

As a child, I was always interested in metaphysical subjects and anything weird, or different. As soon as I heard of anything that I might be interested in, I just *had* to go and find out more about it. As I learned, I became aware of more information that I did not know, which led to more study. My mind was on fire. However, the late 1950s was a very conservative era in the country and there was not much information available, especially to a child of the era.

I hated school for the most part, though I did love art, music, and science. Those were the only subjects that I truly cared about, but I was always an avid reader. I got along with most of the kids, but I was sort of a loner. On more than one occasion, when I asked a girl to play with me, she would say, "No, I don't want to play with you, you're different." So I basically mostly played by myself, though it never bothered me. I remember another girl asked me, "Don't you just love school?"

"No" I said, "I hate it! I hate being told what to do!" I guess honest comments like that kept me being far from popular.

All the kids at school could not wait to grow up. I was in no rush to because it seemed to me that all the grownups were generally in a bad mood most of the time and I wanted nothing to do with *that*.

One TV show I loved back then was "One Step Beyond," which dealt with strange, but true, stories of a metaphysical bent.

My Uncle Eddy, Nana's brother, was a very nice and interesting man, and he would drop by the house for a visit from time to time. He was my favorite uncle. He would entertain Nana and me at the kitchen table with stories about interesting subjects he saw on television. Shows that were different than the ones my family watched. Once he told us about the Abominable Snowman from the Himalayan Mountains in Asia. I was instantly fascinated and pressed him for more information.

Through him, I learned of UFOs as well. This was a hot topic back then and it seemed that the skies were full of them at the time. Looking back, I can see how and why my psychic Nana, and her brother, and I had such a close association and spoke of many unusual and interesting subjects. They both were more open than most people when it can to understanding and being interested in, things of a non-linear nature. Oddly, Mom always left the room when we got onto subjects like that.

Nana's husband, my grandfather Pop, used to wake up in the pre-dawn very early regularly. Sometimes, I would wake up and hear the sounds of him making coffee and I would sneak downstairs through the dark house to talk with him. He was always fun. We talked about all sorts of things, and I always enjoyed his company. One morning he told me about his experience of sitting alone having his morning coffee, when suddenly he felt someone poke him right in the middle of his back with one finger. He turned around, but there was no one there. This had happened to him every now and then. His most recent experience had been that very morning. This information had been relayed to me in a very matter of fact way, as if there was not a thing frightening at all, nor anything of any concern. I got very excited right away and wondered aloud if it were either his parents or brothers, all of whom had already died. Maybe they were saying "hi" to him. His reaction was to say he did not know who it was and treated it as nothing irregular had happened. Eventually, we talked of other subjects, but I never forgot about that morning.

Our talk was eventually interrupted as it always was, by family members coming downstairs as the sun rose.

I was lucky to have grown up in an area, although suburban, that had many acres of open woods to play and hangout in. I have always been in love with nature and the woods and considered myself part of it. My sun sign is Taurus. Its element is the earth, so for me it was a natural thing to practically spend most of my time there.

In the free childhood days of the 1950s I was gone from home for hours at a time playing with other children. Sometimes, I played alone, but mostly in the woods with no fear. I have always felt peacefully at home and safe in the woods. I know everything I need to survive with is in the woods as the Native Americans did. I do not feel good in most large cities, as there is too much energy, both good and bad, for me to feel comfortable in.

In time, the ghost lights that I saw at home at night started to scare me. I now know the reason why I was afraid is because as I grew up, I had learned to believe in the 3D world I was presently living in, as a real thing. My mind was no longer able to casually accept lighting without electrical wiring. It started to scare me, and I wanted not to see so much clairvoyantly. As the saying goes, "Watch out for what you ask for, you might just get it." I lost my clairvoyant ability and tuned into feelings instead. That is, clairsentient. One Who Feels Clearly, and a Psychic Knower. I also started to hear the Still Small Voice Within much, much more. What I always called from my earliest memories, The Voice. I noticed very soon that the more I listened to, and paid attention to, and took the advice it offered, that only good things would come to me as a result. It has never led me astray or frightened me. I learned by paying attention and follow its advice and I could choose to ignore it all I want, but to do so always leads to a loss for me, or a bad outcome so I listen and act accordingly. The Voice does not sound male or female, it sounds neutral. It just *is*.

When I was less than ten years old, it told me of many native plants that were safe to eat. I was led to Purslane, Yellow Wood Sorrel, and of course, wild fruits and berries. I tried to get my friends to sample them, but they were afraid and thought I was a bit mad.

I now find it amusing how anthropologists surmise how early man learned which plants were good or bad to eat and use. They have come up with theories such as watching what other creatures eat, or trial and error. I believe they were told through their shaman, who was a person who used his own natural psychic powers, to know what is good to eat. Everyone is psychic; they just don't know they are. Perhaps that person heard their own Voice within, leading them on the right path.

Some people call The Voice the Higher Self, or the God Voice. You are free to call it

by any name you wish, as long as you are comfortable with the label you give it.

As I said, I went to Sunday school at the local First Presbyterian Church. I must admit, I was far from a devout, scholarly, well-behaved attendee at Sunday school. I tended to take it all with a grain of salt and be disruptive, but I liked the singing part. Before the age of ten, I had decided I was alternately an atheist, then an agnostic. On the other hand, I used to ask Mom to read me stories out of her Bible when I was in the mood. I would quietly mull it over in my mind on my own. I personally found this more fulfilling than actual Sunday school classes. Eventually, I came around to believing in God.

When the day came that I was presented with my own copy of the Bible by the church, I was very happy, for now I could study and read the Bible on my own. My favorite part was the 23rd Psalm and the words of Jesus.

As my brothers and I grew, we attended Sunday school weekly and when we became old enough, we attended confirmation classes to prepare us to become actual members of the church. My two older brothers were already members.

I started attending my own confirmation classes when I was thirteen. We met once a week on Wednesday nights at the church. The minister taught the class.

One evening, the minister explained what our final exam would be like. First, there was to be the usual question and answer test. Second, we had to write on both sides of a piece of paper why we wanted to join the church. That second part troubled me. I had never thought about why I wanted to join the church. I just had always taken it for granted. My two older brothers had joined, as did Pop and our mother too. My father has a non-practicing Catholic, and Nana a non-practicing Methodist. So why did I want to join? I actually had no idea. That started an intense few days of introspection and contemplation for me. I came to realize that I really did not *want* to join the church. I was simply going along with family tradition.

I believed in God. I already studied the Bible on my own. I just felt that I did not know where I wanted to go with religion. I spoke of this to Mom. She said that if I did not want to attend confirmation class that I did not have to. I was relieved.

Soon after, I came home from school and Mom told me that the minister had called and was wondering why I had missed the last class. She told him what I had said. He then told Mom that he wanted me to come to his office the very next day at the church to have a talk with him after school. My heart sank. I dreaded going to see him. I imagined he would try to scare me into submission with warnings of hell and brimstone and an angry, vengeful, God. I slept badly that night.

The next day at school my stomach was in knots. I crossed the street to the church with trepidation. I knocked on the door to the minister's office, entered, and sat in a chair opposite to him at his desk. We talked. He asked me about how I felt about joining the church. With a trembling voice, I began to explain exactly how I felt and believed, my voice getting stronger as my inner fears subsided. Then he said something that amazed me. He suggested that I read books about other religions

and then to take time and see what worked for me personally. He told me I could continue to attend Sunday school or not, my choice. Plus, that no matter what, I would always be welcome at the church regardless of what religion I decided to join, or even not join. I left the building elated. No angry, judgmental God, or minister! I was free!

The next day I went to the town library and took out several books about other religions and religious history as well. My interest in religion has never abated. With study, I came to the personal conclusion that all religions per se, are valid, but not for me. Many were too full of requirements to make me happy. I felt that God was supposed to be loving and not judgmental nor needy, requiring nothing from anything or anybody. Eventually, I came to the conclusion that spirituality is of God, as opposed to organized religion, which is of man. (Didn't someone say, "Render to Caesar what is Caesar's and render to God, what is God's."?) Perhaps, deep down, I am a gnostic. Regardless, I never attended the Presbyterian Church again.

Chapter 3
A Teenager

Years went by and times changed. Society became more progressive and open to new concepts. Jackie Robinson opened the door for Black Americans to enter into professional sports teams that had been segregated previously. Rosa Parks refused to give up her seat to a white man because she was tired. The Civil Rights movement began, led by Dr. Martin Luther King, Jr. President Kennedy started the Space Race and averted World War III during the Cuban Missile Crisis. It seemed that the mass mind was beginning to expand and evolve. Beatniks were the latest subculture and minds were beginning to open. There were more and more books being written about paranormal and metaphysical subjects.

These books brought ever-increasing knowledge and awareness to mankind, as well as to me. See recommended books/info at end.

About this time, my family and I were watching the news at night when we saw film of four girls from the village of Garabandal in Spain who had visions of the Virgin Mary and the baby Jesus. They were filmed with their heads thrown back looking up in adoration and in trance. It showed them running backward over extremely uneven rocky paths without looking to find their way or stumbling down. We were amazed at what we saw. I, for one, never totally forgot about it, and wondered and pondered it in my heart for years afterwards.

I started attending junior high school. One day, a new girl showed up at one of my morning classes. Then she showed up at an afternoon science class, one of my favorite classes. The teacher was a bit of a quirky type, which made his class fun. I asked her, "Are you in this class?" she nodded, so I retorted, "Your poor kid!" We hit it right off immediately and from that day on, we were inseparable.

Her name was Bari and she came from California with her mom and her British stepdad. She and I were both very much the same: fun, quirky, intelligent, and extremely interested in anything and everything paranormal. We spent many hours engrossed in conversations about anything and everything. I confess that metaphysics and parapsychology were a large part of our conversations, though. She had pamphlets from the British Psychical Society, which she lent me. It was obvious to me that the Brits were far more open to, and advanced in, paranormal subjects than the Americans. I have noted a pattern of dis-information in the United States that has continued to the present, for the most part.

One of our favorite places to hang out was the public library where we would spend whole afternoons looking up subjects we were interested in. There, I learned of Edgar Cayce, called the Sleeping Prophet, because when he gave a psychic reading, he laid down, closed his eyes, and went into a trance. His first readings were strictly medical readings, but he learned he could branch out to include life readings. He taught that "Thoughts are things" and "The mind is the builder."* I did not understand exactly what he meant, but both phrases stuck with me and I kept thinking of them for years, trying to understand. I put them away and never forgot.

I trusted I would eventually come to the knowledge. It was through these books that I learned of reincarnation and life between lives. Bari and I taught each other what we learned and so we grew alongside each other together in wisdom.

We promised each other that whoever died first would contact the other to prove that death was, indeed, not the end.

One day, I remembered an old ouija board in the attic that had been a Christmas present to someone in the family years ago. Apparently, they did not care for it and it had been discarded to the attic. Bari and I got it and brought it to my room for fun and information. At the time, I thought it was harmless fun, but later I learned my innocent assumptions were wrong, indeed.

My friendship with Bari continued for more than three years as we went from junior high into high school. In our freshman year, Bari's stepfather's job at British Rails transferred him to England and the family had to move. We tearfully bade each other goodbye, but we kept in touch through letters and cards.

One letter I will never forget. In it, Bari told me of a psychic woman she had met in the U.K. She told the woman about me and my innate psychic knowledge. The woman told Bari that I am what is now known as a star child, a being who is not of this world, but of a higher plane and other planets. Also, I had chosen to come to earth for a specific purpose, and that when the time was right, I would come to know what that purpose was and then to accomplish it. This information blew me away. (Imperfect me, a star child?) This was another piece of information that I put away for keeping in my mind and heart to try to understand it all.

Decades later I came to the realization that Bari and I were meant to meet and help each other along our respective paths and that we came from the same home group on the other side, also known as heaven. A home group is a group of souls that, regardless of their earthly 3D lives, always get back together when they go home after physical death. They all were sort of born together when the morning stars sang when they were created together at the same time. They learned and grew together through untold centuries. A soul may visit other groups, but home is home.

Losing my friend Bari left a great emptiness inside for a while as we had been virtually inseparable, but I continued on with my paranormal and religious studies while attending high school.

My sojourns to the library continued. There I found a book about yoga written by a Hindu Swami from India. It was not only about hatha (physical) yoga, which is more well known in the west, but also the meditative side of it, which I became very interested in after I discovered it. I spent many hours sitting on the dining room floor in my home in full lotus position meditating when the house was empty and silent. I had discovered meditation before my adored Beatles, so when they, particularly George, discovered the joys of Indian culture, I was all in on that. One sentence from the yoga book that struck me was, "The mind is like a monkey jumping from tree to tree." After more than fifty years, I am still attempting to still that rascal monkey, but oh, those wonderful moments when he sleeps! Meditation has kept me in a good place ever since and has brought me peace and the ability to deal with the trials of life.

My experiments with the ouija board continued with other friends. In time, I discovered that I could use it all by myself and I was using it on a daily basis for hours at a time. I thought it was wonderful that I was growing so "advanced" in my use of it.

One evening, alone in my room, I was doing my math homework while sitting in my chair. I suddenly got the feeling that someone was looking at me. I looked up and I saw my first shadow person. It literally looked like the shadow of a person with no person attached to it. Like a shadow, it was dark, and I could see through it. It was standing about seven feet away from me the across the room opposite me and in front of the far wall. I knew it was looking at me. I sat there and stared at it for a few seconds looking at it without emotion, almost not believing it was real. It looked back at me. Then suddenly, it turned to its right, did a few prancing steps, and disappeared through the wall on my left! Did I mention my bedroom was on the second floor? When I realized it was real, I got very frightened. I opened the door to the central hall of the house and ran down the stairs. Almost at the bottom, I could see into the living room on the left and the family inside watching TV. Mom was next to the door on the left and closest to me. She must have seen the fear on my face. She asked, "What's the matter?"

"Nothing," I answered quickly. I then ran off to the kitchen to get control of myself and to think the matter over. Frankly, I was afraid to go back to my room.

Frantically I racked my brain trying to make sense of it. *What was it? Where did it come from? Why was it staring at me?* I got myself something to drink and joined everyone in the living room.

I hesitantly went back upstairs to my room when the rest of the family went upstairs to bed. I peered into my room. No shadow person. I reluctantly went to bed afraid it would return. Somehow, I slept. Next morning, I knew what I had to do. I took that ouija board and threw it directly into the trash container outside! I knew in my heart I never should have used that ouija board like it was a toy, as it is marketed. It is a multi-dimensional tool as dangerous as a gun with no safety!

The average person cannot see spirit people and they are ignorant of what these beings are capable of when calling them in for fun and thrills.

On a much more positive note, at about that time in my life I learned from personal experience that our prayers will be answered, and I guess not by chance.

I had a friend from school who was also in the school chorus with me. One day she asked me if I was interested in singing in the junior choir at her church. It was a local Methodist Church and it turned out that many of the kids I had already knew from school as well and liked them. The members of the junior choir had little monthly social parties hosted by the church on church grounds. In case of bad weather, they were held inside. I would have to go to rehearsals once every week on Wednesday evenings. Also, on Sundays we would do a quick run-through before services. Then we put on our choir robes and walk into the sanctuary while singing in time to the organ. We had to stand and sing whenever it was time again to sing, and we then walked out singing at the end as a group. I also would have to go to their Sunday school. I did not mind the Sunday school part, though I already had my own opinions about organized religion, which I did explain to the minister beforehand just how I felt and he said it was all right with him. I did not go with any sort of religious ideations, just social. I joined and I did have fun and got along with everyone. It even turned out that the church was the same one Nana had gone to as a girl herself.

I also had a profound spiritual experience there. One Sunday's sermon was about God offering Solomon anything he wanted, and that He would give it to Solomon, whatever it was. Solomon requested only knowledge and understanding. The minister described in great detail about the incredible goodness of Solomon in asking for such simple things. He also spoke of how truly compassionate and altruistic, yet so humble. He then, in particular, commented at great length on the goodness of an understanding heart.

I had heard many sermons before, but this one touched me heart, mind, and soul. I had to fight back the tears that came to my eyes, sitting up there at the front of the entire congregation. I thought about it all day. Before I slept that night, I prayed to God honestly and humbly and asked to be granted a compassionate and understanding heart.

God not only gave me what I asked for, but he also gave me a drive to learn to understand the all, including God. As Moses said, "I want to know that God is God." Understanding has always helped me to see the other side of a problem, idea, positive or negative. It keeps me wisely careful and I am humbly grateful for the blessing of the answer to my prayer.

After about six months in the choir, the minister took me aside and suggested that since I was in the choir and attended functions there, perhaps I should consider joining the church. I told him I would get back to him later. That was the end of that for me as I had decided since I had not joined one church, why join another? I felt no need of it. I had my connection to God already. So I left the Methodists.

My studies of the paranormal continued unabated with careful caution. I got a part-time cashier job, which gave me the money to join a metaphysical book club. It was a great source of information for me. I studied subjects such as kabbalah, astrology, scrying, reincarnation, and much more.

One of my favorite books was about witchcraft. It covered not only the history of the craft, but also taught the reader how to actually become a witch. I personally did this rite, which included taking the witch's vow and a witch name. I can never divulge this name to anyone, except another witch. I learned there were both good (white) and bad (black) witches, males and females.

The book also contained spells. There were spells for simple subjects such as to bring luck, love, prosperity, and happiness. There were also spells for darker things such as attacking someone psychically, and making someone sick, or even worse. The most negative one was "How to Conjure a Demon." Even the author, himself, warned against even attempting it. While reading about this, the voice rather loudly told me not to mess around with it. The warning was so strident that I never read it.

I was still interested in the craft, however. From the book I learned how to make a personal talisman for protection, which entailed writing out your personal spell on a piece of paper, wrapping it in cloth, consecrating it with a flame, and putting it away for safekeeping. I was particularly drawn to playing with the flame with my fingers and making up little spells of my own, most of a positive nature.

I did, however, perform one negative spell. I had a teacher at school who I really did not like at all. I decided to cast a spell on her. I just wanted her gone from school, but not dead. I wrote up a spell on paper, writing it in a language that I did not speak. At the time I did not know how I was able to do this, but I did not care, I just performed it. It seemed natural to me at the time. It is only now, years later, that I learned I was subconsciously tapping into a past life when I was a witch. I was replaying it back again in the twentieth century. I simply followed my inner memory on the writing and spell casting. The spell stated that the person would get very, very sick, almost unto death. Then come back to health. (My voice was very strident about the coming back part!)

Very soon the teacher was not at school anymore. I realized that witchcraft and spell casting were not just casual fun and games. It was real! It happened *exactly* as I said it would! It turned out she was gone for almost the entire school year. I felt guilty for having cast that spell. I was relieved that I had not cast a spell for her death, as was my original intent, as I would then have her death on my head. I resolved from that moment on, to never perform a negative spell again. I am strictly a white witch, who works only for the good of all.

One day I was wondering and meditating about life in general. People are born, grow up, have families of their own, age, then die. Then I looked to the future of generation, after generation life after life, endlessly. According to my understanding at the time, reincarnation somehow fit into all of this. I could see no logical reason for it all. It seemed so futile. Then I thought to myself and asked within, "What's it all for then, what's the point? Why do we live life after life?" Immediately, the voice said, "Spiritual growth." I then had an ah-ha moment and understood. I now finally, had something tangible to work for and my personal soulic growth became the most important aspect of my life forever.

One day, my brothers and I were discussing what our earliest memories were. Mom was nearby listening. When it came my turn, I told of my first memory, of that hot summer day so many years ago. When the men were applying aluminum siding on the house and Nana brought out glasses of cold lemonade for everyone's refreshment.

Mom piped in, "You couldn't have remembered that, you weren't born yet! I was pregnant with you at the time." We were all surprised. I remembered that fact and realized that what I had read from the Edgar Cayce readings years ago in the library was indeed true and that we do visit home to familiarize ourselves with our home surroundings prior to physical birth. So my second earliest memory of life was actually my first! I was remembering visiting home prior to actually being physically born! As for Mom and my brothers, I think they put that away deep inside themselves. Ha!

I continued with school and my side studies as time passed. I started to date boys, getting into the physical side of life as opposed to the metaphysical, as young adults do according to the pre-programming of their genes, which is part of life in the third dimension.

I had a steady boyfriend named Bob and, like any other young couple, we sought out private places for romance. One evening, we walked across the train tracks to get to a small natural beach I knew of along the river. While crossing the tracks, Bob easily walked ahead as I followed. Then, a train's headlight appeared down the tracks, far away, but approaching. I stared at the light as I was caught in it. I saw nothing but the light, suddenly, the scene changed. I found myself in a compound surrounded by barbed wire. It was night and a very bright searchlight enveloped me. I heard a man yell, "Halt!" then I heard the sound of a machine gun and felt bullets hitting my body. I thought I heard someone, at the same time, very far away shouting "Linda" at me. The next instant, my boyfriend grabbed my arm and yanked me off the tracks, barely missing the train as its whistle screamed as it passed us by.

He asked me why I stared at the train and I told him I was not sure why. Then I told him about what I saw and heard. He thought I was crazy. I knew I was not. With introspection and meditation, I came to remember that I was killed tying to escape from a German prison camp during the 1940s. I feel I was a POW then.

One day after school, I was standing on Main Street and a girl walked past me and exclaimed, "Linda!" It was my long-lost friend, Bari! We hugged and kissed each other and jumped up and down with joy. Her stepfather had been transferred back to the U.S.! We went right to her new home and got reacquainted.

We quickly fell into talking about our favorite subject, the paranormal. Bari showed me a way to tap into my past lives. I reclined on her bed. I do not exactly remember what she did, but she lastly touched my forehead to open my third eye to see clearly. After a few quiet minutes, I found myself standing in a stone courtyard. Directly ahead of me was a stone pyramid with a stairway going up the side of the pyramid's middle. There were stone buildings surrounding the courtyard. I saw no people anywhere. I walked to the pyramid and started climbing the stairway. I was afraid. I arrived at a platform built into the side of the pyramid. Before me was a large, heavy, rough-hewn wooden door. Seeing that door filled me with dread. I knew I had to go through that door, but I was afraid to. I wanted to escape, but I could not, I *had* to go through that door. I had never been so scared before or after. I was just about to touch the door when I suddenly sat up and quit the vision. I could not take it. Bari was surprised and a little angry at my reaction. I told her about what I saw, and she said I should have gone through the door and that she was disappointed. I was not. I was not ready yet to look at that particular experience yet.

Eventually, after graduation we went our own separate ways. Bari moved to the west and I got married. Decades later, we found each other again through social media but we had both followed our own path in life and had grown up and our time for being close young girls in this life was over.

* Edgar Cayce quote: 281-39

Chapter 4

2nd Decade

I married my old steady boyfriend Bob at the age of eighteen. A year and a half later, I found myself pregnant. I was extremely ill from morning sickness and had to quit working less than one month into my pregnancy. So I was now a full-time housewife, which of course, gave me lots of time for paranormal studies. Even better, I now lived less than a mile from the library for study.

Once a week, on Mom's day off, she and my Nana would pick me up in Mom's car and we would go shopping together. One morning, when I was seven months pregnant, we were all together in the car with myself in the backseat while Mom was driving, and Nana was in the passenger seat. They were talking away while I was lost in thought. I was thinking about time and space and wondering how it all worked. I knew that we, here on earth measure our days by the earth's revolution creating day and night. A year is measured by the completion of an orbit of the earth around the sun. A century is one hundred of the earth's solar revolutions.

However, I surmised, if a person were to get into a rocket and go into space away from our planet and solar system how would they have a twenty-four hour day, or a year, or a century? How about in a different solar system or a different galaxy?

Instantaneously, my entire field of vision was filled with a bright white light! I saw nothing else and I heard nothing. Suddenly, I understood without words that time and even space, as we know it here on earth, does not exist at all. It is a mental construct (that is, an idea) that humankind had decided en masse together for convenience to order their lives by, while living here on earth. I realized there is only the eternal here and now! Immediately, just as suddenly as the vision occurred, it disappeared. I found myself back sitting in the car's back seat and Mom and Nana were in the front talking. They were obviously unaware of my experience. I was amazed that they had not at least seen the light, but it apparently was just for me. I decided to put it away for another time for reflection, and I learned and retained…

My son Christopher was born a month before I turned twenty-one. When my little son was placed in my arms for the first time, I experienced a sense of awe. It was amazing to me that this perfect little being had grown within my body. He quickly became the center and love of my life.

One day, when Chris was less than a month old, I was holding him in my arms after feeding him. I looked lovingly at him and said, "Little soul, how far have you come to be with me now?" I was in a relaxed and open frame of mind, but I received no answer or inkling. I knew then, it was not for me to know at that time. It was just time for me to be a mommy.

Decades later, when my son was grown into a fine and good man and was independent, I occasionally would have a slip of the tongue and refer to him as "my brother," and I would correct myself right away. This happened many times for years and I would jokingly tell people, "I guess he might have been a brother to me in a past life!" After a while, I came to the conclusion that he had, indeed, been my brother in a past life, though I cannot remember specifically anything from any particular incarnation. Only when I was truly ready inside was I ever able to remember specific past lives. I am content with the small hints I have received from within in this life; as I know all will be remembered when this body I now inhabit dies and I go home to the other side (heaven).

My marriage lasted only six years. I chose not to request alimony from the court as I, personally believe that since I did not want my husband in my life, then I was not morally obliged to take his money. I felt he owed me nothing. I chose not to live in fear of insufficiency. I believed I would always have enough to get by, and I did. I did, however, take a small amount of money from him for child support for our son. So I went back to work! I was blessed to have Nana and Pop babysitting Chris during the day for free. I did not have much money, but I got by and made good friends and had family nearby and I continued with my studies after work in the evenings.

However, Bible studies began to be more and more important to me and, as a result, I began to believe in religious requirement, which led me to be fearful of sin and judgment. As a direct result of these beliefs, I threw out my entire collection of books about metaphysics and started to attend a local non-denominational evangelical church. This did not last long, however, as the voice spoke to me during one of my periods of introspection and gently and lovingly said within, "You know deeply that there is more to God than anger and judgment. Stay with love, forgiveness, and listening within and you will be fine."

It was a challenge to make a permanent break from organized religion, but I trusted the voice and knew it never lied to me and it always led me to goodness and blessings, so I made the break and immediately started to grow more and more spiritually aware and became increasingly psychic very quickly, as if to make up for lost time. At this time, I still did not yet have a personal relationship with God.

I do respect the world's religions. Religions are a socially acceptable theological and spiritual teaching service for people. Some people like or need the ritual associated with it. Everyone has an inborn need for spirituality. Each religion is one of many tools for spiritual/psychic study. People are drawn to this information instinctively because everyone is already part of God and everything else. All people have an innate connection to God and the infinite, regardless of culture. The basic tenets of all religions are the same. They are one at heart.

One negative incident that I experienced for which I had no prior inkling of was an auto accident that I was in at the age of twenty-seven. It was the worst, most emotionally painful experience of my life to date but ultimately a great teaching experience. It was a life-changing event for not only me.

I was driving home from work. It was in the middle of the week between Christmas and New Year's. I was in a very happy mood. Chris and I had just had a very happy Christmas the weekend before. I was looking forward to going ice-skating with him and some friends that evening. I was singing happily to myself while driving along to pick up Chris at Mom's place as I did daily after work. The road veered to the right and as I turned, a woman came into my field of vision walking from left to right. I slammed on the brakes, but the car did not stop in time. The unfortunate was hit head on and went up against the windshield. I was horrified! At that point, the car came to a stop and she disappeared from my view.

My first instinct at that moment was escape, but the voice literally screamed at me, "Do *not* run! If you do, it will be all the worse for you! You must stay and take it!" (Until this day, I feel for the drivers of hit and runs. It is instinctual to want to escape from such a horrific incident.)

I froze. People were running to the event from all sides. I got out of the car, looked down, and to my horror, the woman was lying on the ground directly in front of my car. I realized with horror that had I taken off in my car that I would have driven over her! A few yards away, her son stood transfixed. He had been walking across the street with his mom when the accident occurred. He seemed numb too. I felt immediate compassion for him.

Then I saw a man put his coat on the hapless woman and I thought, "That's a good idea," so I did the same with my own coat.

The New York State Police and the ambulance arrived quickly. She was taken to the hospital. The crowd dispersed. I was left standing there with the police alongside of me. One officer asked me, "Where's your coat?" as I stood there shivering in the cold wind.

"On the lady to keep her warm." I replied with a quivering voice, trying to hold back my tears. They both looked at each other and then at me with pity and kindness and then one offered to let me warm up in their car. The instant I got in the back seat, I exploded hysterically crying and screaming out, "Oh God! Let her live! Let me die! Take my life and let her live! Let her live, please!"

I pleaded over and over and cried to God until I had cried myself out. I had no idea how long I went on. When I finally quieted down, the police got into the car and asked where I had been heading prior to the accident. I explained to them that I was going to pick up my son after work at my mom's house a mile away. They told me they were going to drop me off there as we rode in the patrol car down the street. I was surprised by their answer. I asked them with a small voice, "Aren't you going to take me to jail?"

Again, that kind look of compassion flashed across their faces when they looked at each other at what I said and one said, "No, there has not been an investigation yet." I was amazed. I had hit a person with my car, and they were taking me to my mother's house? I felt so guilty and awful. Then they told me to stay there and wait for a detective to arrive to talk to me.

At the house I was let out of the patrol car and went inside with dread. How could I tell my family what had happened, but how could I not? I walked from the living room into the kitchen. Mom, Nana and Pop, Chris, and my younger brother were all seated at the table having dinner. Mom turned to me smiling, saying in a happy, teasing way, "Now what made you so late?" I blurted out what had happened and burst into tears. Mom jumped to her feet and put her arms around me for comfort. I cried very much. Somehow, the time passed until the detective came by. He brought my coat from the hospital and handed it to my mom. We all saw blood on it. Mom grabbed it and folded it up said, trying to hide the obvious from me, "I want to wash it, there is dirt on it."

I said, "Mom I saw the blood. That's not dirt." Seeing that made me feel all the worse because it was obvious that the lady had been severely injured.

The detective informed us that the woman was in surgery at the time. Then, as on cue, the phone rang. I answered, and the caller asked to speak to the detective. He spoke briefly on the phone and then hung up. He looked disappointed and seemed obviously sorry for me. He told us that the lady had died on the operating table and as a result that I would have to go to the state police station to be interviewed for the investigation. He told me that she had been a divorcee with three children. As a divorced mother myself, my sense of guilt was overwhelming. Her children were now motherless. I felt shame.

Mom went with me to the police barracks, but I had to go alone into the interrogation room. The detective had me tell him all about the accident many, many times. I felt there was not much to tell. I had taken the life of an innocent person who did not deserve to die. I felt so guilty and low. I felt I deserved to be prosecuted to the fullest extent of the law because I had killed someone. Someone who had three children who needed and loved their mother.

Finally, when I was re-telling the tale one last time, I described my first sight of her prior to the accident as walking across the road while looking down and swinging her purse. This was a memory I had forgotten. The detective's eyes widened with excitement when he heard me recount this memory as it basically proved the occurrence to be a simple accident and not my fault.

I must add for the record that I experienced nothing but kindness from all the New York State Police that I met that night. They are good people who just want to do right, for my part, anyway.

I got to go home with Chris that night, but I had a court date to go to. I had never been to court before except when divorcing my former husband. When my turn came and the judge asked me how I pled, I said, "Guilty," as I felt I was. The judge cautioned against that and said that if I were found guilty that I would have to either pay a one thousand dollar fine or do one year in jail. My heart sank. However, the judge gave me a court appointed lawyer as I was just barely getting by financially. In the end, I only had to pay a fine, but I never really got over it. For a full year afterwards, whenever I thought about that night, I would cry. In time, I learned to live with it.

If it were not for my personal beliefs and spirituality, I am sure I would have become severely depressed, even suicidal. I had learned prior to the accident about how our lives and life experiences are like a chain with each link representing an important incident in our respective lives. Each link is important. I was the last link in her chain. The incident left me with a great sense of personal responsibility. I would never again look at life as a light-hearted, frivolous romp.

Another incident occurred in my pivotal twenty-seventh year of life: I met my dearest and longest friend, MaryAnn. She was a sixteen-year-old wild child who was a mass of bubbly, fun energy who I liked immediately. We hit it right off. A farm girl whose intelligence was innate: she was no book worm like me, but like a sponge, her mind readily sucked up anything I ever taught her about metaphysics or parapsychology.

As the years passed and I continued with my studies, I taught her all I knew and everything I learned. At the time, she called me a "walking, talking book."

By the time of this writing, we have been friends for more than forty years and we have seen each other through lovers, husbands, children, deaths, and births. She is amazingly wise and one hell of a horsewoman. I could not imagine life without her. Our meeting was no accident and I know it was a pre-set from our life between lives.

My studies continued through my twenties as I again began acquiring books on metaphysics, paranormal, and spiritual subjects, but I kept wondering about that quote from Edgar Cayce, "Thoughts are things." I knew it was important. I did not understand exactly how that concept worked, but I felt it was important, and I learned and retained…

Chapter 5
3rd Decade

Just seven months after my thirtieth birthday, I met Rudy, my second husband. There was no doubt in either of our minds that we were meant to meet and come together at that particular time and place. Like me, he was a sensitive and psychic.

He had just returned back home to the northeast the day before I met him. He had been living in California for the past ten years. Suddenly, one day, he *knew* he had to leave and go back east to home, so he packed up his necessities, quit his job, and took off in this Volkswagon Fastback.

For my part, I had decided to take Mom out for a drink for my first and only time of my life. I was temporarily living with her and Nana after the break-up of a relationship. Pop had died while I was in my twenties.

The first place Mom and I went to visit was totally packed, so we went to another place. When we entered, we saw two seats on the opposite side of the square bar. I sat with Mom on my right and a man I did not know on my left. He said to us, "Good evening, ladies," with a smile. We wished him the same and returned to our conversation. Undaunted, he then introduced himself as Rudy and the woman on his left as his sister, Mary. He told us he had just returned home to New York from California and was staying at his sister's place until he got a job and a place of his own. I told him I was living at Mom's place temporarily after a break-up and I had decided to take her out for a drink for the first time for us together. He was the most charming man I had ever met.

We all talked and drank for a while, but Mom wanted to leave after her second drink, so I told them reluctantly that we had to leave. He asked me to come back, but I was ambivalent about going back as I did not actually know him. After all, one must be careful! I was very noncommittal and said, "I'll see." He begged me to return.

When Mom and I arrived home, we told Nana about the siblings we had met. Over and over Mom kept talking about what a nice guy he was. Then she said, "You're going back, aren't you?"

"No," I said, "I don't know what kind of person he is." Mom insisted she could tell he was very nice and that I should go right back. So I did.

When I returned he was elated. "You came back, you came back!" he kept repeating. We realty hit it right off and talked for hours. Mary decided to take off with some friends and left us at the bar. I felt so comfortable with him. He was a lot of fun, charming, mellow, kind, personable, and easy to talk to. I felt I could tell him anything.

We talked of paranormal and metaphysical subjects. He told me he could see auras and that mine was mostly white with a bit of gold.

I said, "Me? A white aura?" I did not think I was developed enough to have a white aura. MaryAnn sees auras as well and she always told me my aura looked purple and indigo to her.

Somehow, I ended up at his place. Mary was not home yet. I generally did not sleep with a man the first time I met him, but with Rudy it seemed natural. Afterwards, we fell asleep and I began to dream.

I dreamed we were in Afghanistan centuries ago. I had never seen anything of that country before in my present life, but I knew where I was. Rudy and I shared a secret, forbidden love for each other back then. I was not free to have any relationship with him then, but we had a clandestine one. We decided to run away together. We planned to leave when there was a large market with a big crowd of people around. We planned to be lost in the crowd and disappear. We knew that if we were caught, that we would be killed, but we were willing to take the chance. We failed in our attempt. We were found out and caught and were stoned to death together.

I awoke with a start. Rudy was fast asleep beside me. I knew immediately that that dream was no dream, but a memory of a past life! I went back to sleep.

I dreamed again. I was on the seashore in Medieval England. I was a member of Norman aristocracy. I was wearing a deep green velvet dress with fancy trim. On my head was a very small green velvet skullcap trimmed all around with tiny pearls. My hair was dark and very long and ran down my back. Standing beside me was my servant, who was my secret dear friend, as well. I recognized her as MaryAnn, my friend from this present life. Her dress was much plainer than mine in a simpler style of a dull reddish-brown color. We were having much fun, laughing and talking together. We were practicing falconry. Behind us, on a rise, above the shore, was a large dark looming thing that I recognized as my home then, but it looked like no home or castle I had ever seen in this life and could not identify what it was. Years later, I learned of Mott and Bailey castles and realized just what my home then had been, and it all made sense.

Suddenly, without warning, a Viking ship came up onto the shore right near us making a large noise and frightening us. A large Viking man jumped overboard and ran up the rise to us. He grabbed me and threw me over his shoulder and ran back to the ship taking me aboard. I knew Rudy had been that Viking. The last I saw of my friend was her standing on the shore with her arms reaching out to me, as I sailed away. The dream ended.

I yelled, waking us both up. I told him of my dreams. He did not discount them as they held a ring of truth to him as well.

Three months later, we were married on Valentine's Day. We had many happy years together, and Chris got to have a stepfather he could love and count on.

The second summer of our marriage Rudy's son, Matt, and his stepdaughter, Lisa, came to visit us for a few weeks. After they returned home to the west coast, I often had a vision of Matt wearing an Egyptian collar showing up at my kitchen door. I psychically knew that one day he would return to my life again, as he did before, in ancient Egypt. I even dreamed several times of he and I there conversing, standing near a pyramid, but the pyramid was covered in metal. It was used as a power source, not a burial chamber. At that time Egypt was a colony of Atlantis.

Two years later, he permanently came back into our lives. In the interim, Matt's mom and stepfather had moved to the island of Maui in Hawaii with the kids.

Unfortunately, Matt had really taken with the Hawaiian lifestyle in a bad way. According to his Mom, he was impossible to discipline. He habitually skipped school. Apparently, marijuana grows literally like weeds everywhere there and he was constantly stoned as well as doing nothing but surfing and hanging out on the beach. If his mother or stepfather attempted to discipline him, he would sneak out and sleep on the beach.

Matt's mom gave Rudy two choices: Matt could either come to live with us permanently or he would be sent to a facility. She had had enough and was at her wits end. For Rudy, there was but one choice: Matt would live with us.

Before Matt arrived, Rudy and I had a talk. Matt would have to live by the same rules that Chris had to abide by. Rudy had no problem with this idea as I was always an understanding and fair disciplinarian.

So Matt came to live with us. Rudy and I decided not to lay down any rules at the onset and not to be confrontational and to deal with things as they came up. He started attending the local high school and came right home after school every day. No problems. One evening after dinner, he went to go out to see some friends from school. I said to him, " You can go out, but before you do, I need to know where you are going, who you are going to be with, and when you are coming home."

He retorted calmly, "I don't have to tell you that."

I calmly said, "Oh no? Well, I'll tell you what, Chris has to abide by the same rules.

Don't you, Chris?" He nodded. "I expect nothing more from you than I do from my own son. Your mother sent you to live with us because she can't handle you anymore. You have no choice, it's living here with us, or a home. I could choose to take the easy way out and not give a shit what happens to you; you are not my kid, but I *choose* to give a shit. Therefore, I want to know where you are going, who you are going with, and when you will be home." I said this calmly, but firmly. My guts were in a twist. I expected a bad reaction.

He looked at me, nodded his head, said "Okay," and told me everything I wanted to know. I then told him, "Have a good time. See you later."

He never gave me any trouble after that. Was he an angel? No, but neither was my own son, Chris. They were teenagers. To this day, Matt and I are close, and I call him "The Son I Never Gave Birth To" and we still keep in touch and see each other occasionally.

During this time in my life, while driving home from work I would listen to a talk show on the car radio daily. The host would interview all sorts of interesting people. One day, he interviewed a gentleman by the name of Dan

Smith, from the Unarius Academy of Science in El Cajon, California. He spoke at great length about the "Science of Spirituality." This was a new and exciting idea to me! He also spoke of past life therapy, another new concept for me. I was enthralled.

He told of Ernest L. and Ruth E. Norman, the founders of Unarius, and of the books they write and publish to educate mankind to the truth of metaphysics. Mr. Smith also told about how, what people think and believe of as religion, is actually science: energy in action. I was enthralled.

Arriving home from my drive, I ran right into the house to listen to the interview to the end. He gave the address of Unarius and told the public to request an information packet, which I did. This was in the days of no computers and life was slower and we had to wait for physical mail to arrive.

I was absolutely amazed at the amount if information that I received for free! Booklets, pamphlets, and pages upon pages of information that took me weeks to get through, I learned of channeling, the multiverse, how everything is energy, U.F.O.s, and the different people from them and their contact with humanity, and the coming spiritual (energetic) ascension of mankind. There was too much information for me to describe here and I had not yet ordered any books! I was hooked.

After I started to actually study the books themselves, I started to become aware and seeing how my past lives affect my present life. I learned that I was led to the Unarius information when I was developed enough to appreciate and understand it. I learned how to tune into everything and anyone at any time because I was raising my personal frequency and started to be open to the idea of the multi-verse and became able to connect to (remember) past life experiences as a result as well.

Through introspection, I became more aware of the life of privilege and obligation in Old England that I had lived as a princess. I had been resigned to an unhappy life of obligation; my abduction by Rudy, as a Viking then, was an unexpected way out. Then, I had been promised in marriage as a political pawn to a man I did not know. I was not looking forward to it but was resigned to my fate. Although I had resisted being abducted from my home, I came to love him and willingly went with him and other Norse settlers far to the west across the sea. However, the climate changed and turned our home in the new land cold and barren. My husband with the able-bodied men went east for more supplies leaving behind the old, women, and children. The advancing arctic ice prevented their return and we starved and froze to death. I died cursing him, looking out across the icy sea.

I also became much more aware of the voice. I learned from the Unarius books that many members and students hear it regularly and also, like myself, came to know that to ignore it was not in their best interest. So, my hearing the voice was not such an unusual thing at all, and that everyone has access to the voice, not just saints, prophets, and holy men, as most of humanity has been told by organized religions! We are *all* worthy of the voice and direct contact to our higher self, which is an aspect of God.

I feel it extremely important to point out right here and now that the voice is *not* the devil, demons, or anything else bad. The voice is soft and always heard in my right ear. I have myself, never personally experienced it, but if one hears a voice in the left ear it should be ignored. Just as there are good and bad people here in the third dimensional world, there are good and bad entities from both inside and outside of our own dimension. These entities that I speak of here are human ghosts, they once lived on the earth as physical people. There are entities that enjoy doing bad things to people. Bad entities have the ability tell you to do bad things, such as harming yourself and/or others. They can make you feel bad and afraid within. That is not the voice. Tell bad entities to go away the instant you become aware of them and do not listen to them. The voice will only bring you peace and goodness. As protection I surround myself mentally with the white light of heaven daily and I suggest you do the same. I also pray and meditate daily.

There is a negative and a positive side to all things. The negative can try very hard to lead the ignorant innocent awry. The power of God is absolute and if one strives to do only good and loves and forgives all that there is (especially the negative) you will be protected. Meditate and pray daily. Even just five minutes a day works.

I also started getting flashes of intuition as a direct result of my studies. This has helped me tremendously in endless ways, such as making me a better cook by suggesting changes in recipes. All my life I have been an avid cook. Another way that my intuited flashes help is I have been known to suddenly change my route while driving to an alternate route due to "a feeling" I get. Has it had any effect? I guess so, as I don't have accidents. I have also learned to relax and keep open to intuition. Where it leads, I follow. I shall ever be grateful to the Unarius Academy of Science for the knowledge I gained from them, and I learned and retained more than I ever thought possible in one lifetime.

Rudy and I raised our boys together. We also drank together on a daily basis. I could never drink as much as him. It was physically impossible for me to keep up. I started to look at our drinking as a waste of money, not to mention its effect on our health. I could, and did, stop anytime I wanted to, but Rudy was unable or unwilling to do so. My studies continued unabated, however, and I learned and retained as ever.

Chapter 6
4th Decade

Eventually, the boys graduated high school. Rudy's job got sold to a new owner who moved the business to his home in the state of Connecticut. Rudy's drive went from a half hour each way to an hour and a half. This was not feasible, so we decided to move to Connecticut. I got work easily in Connecticut. The boys chose to stay in New York with family members. Rudy's drinking grew more frequent and heavier and progressed into alcoholism. At least, he was not a nasty drunk. My drinking was nil to non-existent for the most part.

I had several different jobs over the years and eventually, I had a job as a night shift supervisor at a local convenience store. My responsibility was mostly the cash handling and minding the store. My female co-worker worked the deli department. We worked midnight until 7 A.M. We got along well and worked together efficiently. Eventually, we became friends.

On one evening, our first day back to work together since the previous weekend, I asked her how she was doing. She said, "Not too well, I have had earaches in both of my ears all weekend. They are killing me, and I can't get them to pop to relieve the pressure!"

I said to her, "Gee, I wish I could do something to help you feel better." as an off-hand caring remark.

We then got busily to work with our respective jobs, as I casually imagined a way to help her somehow. I wondered what I could do to help her in an open, easy way. All of a sudden, I had an inner prompting to put my hands over her ears. I looked outside to make sure there were no customers coming. The lot was empty, so I called her to join me in the office area in the back room. Doing what my prompting told me to do, I told her to sit in the office chair. I stood at her back. I lifted my hands and held them open over her ears, but not touching her. I stood that way for several minutes, heat building up under my hands. By instinct, I felt the heat was beneficial.

She exclaimed, "Oh, my God, my ears are getting hot."

"That's okay, that's what it's supposed to do." I answered. I intuited how to do this procedure by following an inner instinct. Silently, I prayed that no one would come into the store. Thankfully, they did not. A while later, I "felt" it was time to stop. We both went back to our respective work. A few minutes later, she yelled out. I asked her what was the matter and she exclaimed, "My ears both popped at the same time and the pain is totally gone. Thank you for whatever you did!" I was amazed and pleased. I knew it was not I who had performed the healing; it was the energy that I channeled that had healed her. Years later, I learned I had used a Reiki technique, although I had never even heard of it at the time.

My studies continued. Were it not for my studies, or weekend visits from our boys with their future wives, I would have sunk into a very deep depression. I was not happy in Connecticut and I was distressed by Rudy's ever-increasing amount of alcohol that he drank on a daily basis. He drank so much I was ashamed of putting out the recycling bin as it showed for all to see how much alcohol was consumed at our house. At this point, he would drink until he passed out drunk every night.

Sadly, eventually, our marriage fell apart. I had had enough. We divorced after sixteen years of marriage.

I was devastated. I felt I had lost my family. I returned to the Hudson River Valley. I got an apartment and a job and started making new friends and catching up with old ones. Life went on.

Chris lived nearby, which was a comfort, and were other family members in the area.

I made one new friend who was destined to be a big part of my metaphysical life, as well as like a brother to me. He was known as Pirate. Again, one of those rare people I was immediately drawn to on our first meeting. We immediately got down to business discussing metaphysical subjects. I was a white witch. He was a white warlock. He had originally been drawn to the dark side, but came to change his mind. He was very psychic, more than I. We became fast friends. Over the years we had long talks for many hours. We came to realize that we had been together many times over many lives. On more than one occasion we had been brothers in arms and warriors alongside each other and died together at least once. We had been husband and wife in what is now known as Israel during the time of Christ. I learned from him and he learned from me. Most of what I taught him was about living on the "Light" side and the importance of loving others unconditionally. He has been the dearest male friend of my life. Eventually, I came to the realization that he was a teacher of mine on the other side in our life between lives.

One day, while sitting alone on a bar's patio in a relaxed, open frame of mind, I suddenly remembered that I, too, was a teacher on the other side as well. (Not like Pirate, however. It's like he teaches college, and I teach high school.) Instantaneously, my consciousness shot out of my head and was suspended about ten feet above my body! I could still see out of my physical eyes where they were in my head, but I was totally aware that my mind was not in my physical brain. I was in a happy, mildly euphoric sensation after a second of disconcerted strangeness. I was aware of the "me in my mind" being surrounded by an aura of shimmering white light. I calmly remained where I was sitting and eventually the feeling of being tuned into a higher frequency calmed down and dissipated and my mind slowly went back into my head. I then understood that the realization of my being a teacher on the other side raised my base frequency instantly and my body could not, at the time, contain it. Therefore, the mind shot out of the brain in the physical body until I had mentally settled into the realization itself. Only then, could the energies be in-sync and the mind and brain be again reunited in the head. Since I already knew from my studies that we all leave our bodies while we sleep that it was not such a big stretch for me to understand what was occurring and not let fear control my experience. I felt elated and grateful for it.

I continued in my studies and learned and retained. I was almost fifty, living alone and self-supporting. I had just moved into a tiny apartment, which suited me perfectly. I was content and happy.

I had a bartending job that was just minutes from my new apartment. I got to meet many new and interesting people and made friends with many of them. Life was full and good.

It was during this time that Princess Diana tragically died. Like many others, I had been quite taken with her. She seemed like such a dear soul to me. I felt terribly sorry for her boys to have lost their mother at such young ages. On television I watched her funeral procession like millions of others all over the world. I could feel the collective grief. I cried for her.

Perhaps a week afterwards, I asked within, "Show me where she now is." I then psychically saw the "Indigo Place," one of the multiple heavens I had learned about from the Unarius Academy of Science. It looked like a city but was actually a universe of its own. It is a very high frequency place and only highly advanced souls go there after physical death. The main course of study there is spirituality. I was not surprised she was there, as she had so much compassion and did so much to help others from her sincere and loving heart. I had been aware of her high personal evolutionary energy level prior to her death. I did a watercolor painting of my vision as a remembrance.

Through a customer at the bar where I worked, I was re-introduced to a guy I had dated twenty years ago for a year and a half. His name was Francisco, but was called Fran for short. Back in the 70s, we had had a long distance relationship because we lived sixty miles apart. We wrote letters back and forth and only got to see each other every three months or so. He was planning on joining the Air Force and dropped an occasional hint about marriage. I thought things over while he was in basic training. Chris was only six years old then. From the age of two he had been safely and lovingly cared for by Nana and Pop. He had a secure life that I would have to take him away from. He would get thrown into military life, which included moving from place to place, never settling down, and losing friends. I did not have the heart to take him away from the only life he knew. So Fran and I went our separate ways. I never forgot him though. I thought of him on occasion, wondering if he had a passel of kids or what.

When we met again, I was simultaneously working the bar and making lunch for a customer, as I usually did. Fran was always a long-winded talker and he had not changed in that way. I had a burger already cooking on the grill back in the kitchen and I needed to run to take care of it. I excused myself, ran to the back, flipped the burger and dropped the basket of fries into the hot oil. All the extras for the burger were all prepped and ready to go, awaiting said burger. (I'm an efficient cook). I ran back out front to the bar and resumed chatting with Fran. I was aware that the food was cooking however, and I soon told Fran I had to leave and run into the back again. He followed me that time.

We talked as I finished cooking and prepping the food. Then he kissed me. Suddenly, the realization came to me that I still cared very much for him after all those years. I brought out the food to the customer accompanied by Fran. He told me he had to leave soon to fly back to his job in the Air Force. He had been serving for nineteen years and had one year to go before he retired. We exchanged phone numbers and addresses. So, there I was, writing him letters again after nineteen years! We wrote many letters and through those letters, we fell back in love with each other all over again. I visited him twice while he was at his final assignment at Grand Forks Air Force Base. We planned to reunite when he could take leave permanently from the Air Force in North Dakota. I told Pirate much about Fran, sharing our letters and photos with him. He said, "I approve."

Six months passed and Arrival Day for Fran came. Within minutes of him actually walking through my door, the doorbell rang and there stood Pirate! He said, "I knew you were here, I could feel you! Now I'm going to go away and leave you two alone until tomorrow!" He then turned on his heel with a big wink and a smile on his face and left.

Fran and Pirate quickly became close friends. The three of us spent many happy times (and many good meals) together through the years.

Fran met Chris and his wife, Diane. Fran had not seen Chris in twenty years since Chris was six years old. Now he was all grown up at 26 years of age with a wife of his own. We enjoyed their company on many occasions, both at our place and theirs. During this time, Chris and Diane bought their first house. Surprisingly, it was well known to Fran from his youth. The house had been the home one of Fran's school friends. The boy's mother had been a seamstress at the Catholic Children's Home that Fran had lived in as a child and he knew the house well. I believe that there are no coincidences.

Fran and I lived happily, but squeezed in tightly, in my tiny apartment for ten months while we were making plans for a move to Minnesota. Fran had family there, and we were ready for a fresh start.

We bade goodbye to family and friends in the east and drove to Minnesota. Within a week of arrival, I had a job. Fran found one two weeks later.

At first, we were very kindly allowed to stay at his stepbrother's home with his family. He also had an uncle in the area with a family of his own, so we had family there. We quickly found ourselves an apartment of our own. Fran joined a local American Legion Post and we made friends easily with the famously friendly people of Minnesota. Life was good and we were content. I did, however, terribly miss my family and friends back in the Hudson River Valley. Unlike Fran, I was not used to living so far away from people I knew and loved, and my heart ached inside.

To cope with my sense of loss, I kept very, very busy with my studies. I had been aware of the book *Autobiography of a Yogi* by Paramahansa Yogananda since the 1960s. I saw it in many bookstores. On the cover is a photo of the Swami. His deep, dark, luminous eyes I found arresting, but I had resisted reading it for years. Finally, I felt very strongly drawn to it, so I purchased a copy. It was a revelation and it confirmed my personal belief that all religions are one and that there are "Blessed Ones" in all religions, regardless of what mankind has been told of disunity by most organized religious organizations. No single book, until then, had ever touched me so inside, or taught me so much. To this day I consider him my personal guru and call him Master. I became a student of his teachings. He died in 1952 and his body is still incorruptible. It does not just happen to Catholic saints.

I also took a correspondence course titled "Astrology and Parapsychology" and graduated 98.7% and received a special commendation for such a high grade in that course of study. The school is still in business, but no longer provides that particular course. The course of study included astrology, palmistry, scrying, the paranormal, the history of metaphysics, and parapsychology. Also psychometry, spiritualism, dowsing, i-ching, and predicting. One very early project I had to do was to make up a set of ESP cards and learn to read them. I got so good at it I would always get ten out of ten correct! I learned very much from the Stratford Career Institute.

One day, as a work assignment, I had to help man a booth in a large stadium that was holding an exposition for local businesses, followed by a free country music concert afterward. We had free handouts for the public as well as items for sale. Each booth represented a particular local business, and it was an opportunity for free advertising. I arrived early to help set up the booth. On purpose, I had parked my car near a light pole that had a numerical identifier on it far from the stadium so it could be easily found when it was time for me to leave.

By mid-afternoon all the items we had to give away or sell were gone so we were allowed to leave early. Gratefully, I left. However, when I returned to the place I had parked my car, I could not find it. It was now surrounded by thousands of cars. I started to panic, but then I started to talk to myself slowly and quietly in order to calm myself down: I remembered that master yogananda said that if you really need an answer to something, that all you have to do is ask God directly, inside, with a sincere heart and you will get an answer. So I closed my eyes, took some long slow breaths, and thought about what I wanted to say. I then said within, "Please God, I can't find my car. Please help me to find it." I stood there relaxed, with my eyes closed, for a moment. Then I heard the voice say, "Look to your right." calmly I opened my eyes, turned my head to the right, and it was *right there* twenty feet away! I was amazed and grateful. I drove home, thanking God all the way. As far as I was concerned, God and I were pals forever!

So, still I studied, learned, grew, and retained.

Fran and I were married in February 2000 by a judge in the charming Afton Inn on the St. Croix River in Minnesota. His uncle and aunt stood up for us. I made our silk flowers for the ceremony. Our only other guest was one of his best Air Force buddies who came from Wisconsin. It was the smallest, most intimate, and for me, my favorite wedding.

Less than a month later, my grandson, Dylan, was born. So now, we were long distance grandparents. Just like many other members of our generation.

Chapter 7
5th Decade

Ten months later, we moved to the state of North Dakota for a new job for Fran at a local television station in Grand Forks that had been promised. However, upon moving up there and setting up a home, the job that he had been promised had been literally been given away to the boss's son, with no warning to us. We had to tighten our belts and hang in until we found jobs, for which it took us each three months respectively.

By and large, the locals were not the friendliest people I had ever met. So unlike the friendly people who lived just next door in Minnesota! It certainly did not help that my features resembled the Native Americans who lived locally. In the east, native people are looked upon with reverence and respect, not so in North Dakota. To me, they were treated as sub-humans. One day, Fran and I went to a local diner for a meal. We just sat there and were not being served. Fran asked a Latino who worked there as a busser if they were not serving us because of his appearance. He said no, it was because of mine. He said I looked like I had just stepped off the reservation. We went elsewhere and never set foot in that place again.

This was not the first, but the most, obvious passive/aggressive experience I had ever experienced before of being judged by prejudicial, ignorant people. I have chosen to bear them no ill. I forgive them their ignorance. That said, I am in no hurry to ever go back there.

At home as children we had been told that we had Indian in our background. We all always assumed it was Native American, as had Nana, as it came from her side of the family. I had always been proud of this heritage.

Even Native Americans who I met at Pow Wows would ask what tribe I was from. I always told them the Sint Sinks, because they were the local tribe in the area where I grew up.

To add an interesting post-script to my personal trials in North Dakota, in the second decade of the twenty teens I had my genes tested. It turned out that I have no Native American Indian background at all. I am, instead, two percent India Indian! Who knew? I can only laugh.

My job started in March 2000. I was as bartender for the Air Force at the Grand Force Air Force Base at The Club. This was a combination restaurant, ballroom with stage and bar, and a casual dining room. It also had multiple barrooms for enlisted Airmen and Non-Commissioned Officers. It took me less than a week to suspect the building where I worked was very, very haunted with a capital H.

Besides bartending, one extremely important part of my job, which involved military security, was to make sure all doors were locked at final rounds at night while closing The Club before locking up for the night. I had to physically push on each security door to make sure they were locked from the inside. Of course, to open the door, one would simply have to push on the bar in front of the door to open it from the inside. Two of these doors were in the ballroom. One of them was around back of the left side of the stage and hidden behind curtains. The second door was at a right angle to the first one up on a rise three stairs heigh that had a bar and lounge with very comfortable captain's chairs just to the right of the stage. This bar area was called Top Side and ran the entire length of the ballroom's right side. Across from the stage there were two swinging doors with windows in them that led into a large commercial kitchen area's central hall.

The first time I stepped into the ballroom while being shown around and being taught my duties, I could feel an oppressive heaviness in there. Then, when I took the three steps up to Top Side it was absolutely creepy. Next, I looked at the doors to the kitchen where I felt, more than saw, an entity that seemed to like to hang around the doors. I never liked to look at, let alone, go through those doors by myself. The "being" that was there really did not even feel human to me. I was not really afraid of it. It was just extremely creepy, and I wanted nothing to do with it.

The next door I had to secure was in the kitchen area. The kitchen consisted of a long hall with doors off to the sides to specific areas for storage, offices, cooking, dishwashing, and so forth. One of the doors was small and was for outside dairy deliveries. That was the one I had to secure. It was located two thirds of the way down the hall from the two creepy swinging doors at the end that led directly into the ballroom. Late at night with The Club quiet, dark, and closed down, I could feel eyes looking at me through those swinging doors. I remembered the creature I had encountered on my first day at work, and I did not want to look through the windows lest I should see it. Locking the kitchen side door was always an unsettling experience that I felt in the pit of my stomach. One I dreaded and had to do, every night.

A retired Airman named Stu worked at The Club as a handyman. His wife was still active duty Air Force on base. They were a very nice couple. Stu and I soon became pretty good pals. He would show up nightly for beer after his work. One day, not long after my first day on the job, I decided to take a chance and ask him if the place was haunted. He did not answer. About a week later I asked again, and he still did not say. He just had a little smile and said, "Could be." That was all I could get from him then.

Not long after that, I got my own answer about the possibility of ghosts there without having to ask anyone. One of my first duties at the bar every day was stocking up the beer case behind the bar. This bar was located at the opposite side of the building from Top Side. The beer was stored behind the bar in a central walk-in storeroom and cooler that contained anything I needed to stock or run a bar with. One day, while first setting up for the shift, I came out from the back carrying a stack of several cases of beer to find a man standing at the far end of the bar near the door that leads to the central hall of The Club. He looked like any workman anywhere. He was white with brown hair that fell down over his forehead. He was wearing a dark colored tee shirt with a pack of Marlboro cigarettes in the pocket with an unbuttoned plaid flannel work shirt over it, jeans, and tan work boots. He looked just like any ordinary regular working guy standing there. I smiled at him, placed the beer on the bar and I said to him, "I'm sorry, I was in the back getting beer. I didn't see you come in. I'm not opened yet, but I can give you something now and then you can pay me in just a little while when I open." Our eyes met, he gave me a little smile, and vanished. I stood there totally amazed. I had seen filmy ghosts before, orbs, and flashes of light, but this guy looked totally solid and alive, then gone. Instantly. I called out to the man, "Well now I know what you look like!"

I could not wait for Stu to finish his work that day and come in for his usual post-work beer so I could tell him about my experience. I described the man to him, and he said the description fit a man who had worked there. He liked to drink there too, and he said many times that when he died that he would come back and haunt the place. He had actually died less than a year before then. We both agreed that he was still around by choice.

From time to time, I had to work Top Side for large functions. It was usually for retirement ceremonies for Airmen, or a few weddings or large parties. Sometimes, when alone setting up and supplying that particular bar before an event, I would hear someone scooping ice out of the ice-making machine when my back was turned. I would turn around, but I could never see anyone, so I ignored it, as I felt there was nothing to fear. When the room was full of people there was no psychic phenomena. I believe that all the mass life energy of the living people in there, in some way interferes with spirit people being able to manifest. Everything is ultimately just energy anyway.

When I first got my job at The Club, things were not going well financially with us. We had hardly any money and we could barely pay our rent, never mind the bills. No friends, and it seemed to me that the locals were against me, personally. I had tried everything I could think of to make things better for Fran and me to no avail. At the time I was the sole support, except for his monthly Air Force retirement check. There seemed to be nothing I could do to make our life better financially. I could see no way out and I was feeling desperate. One day, as I was driving to work, all of these negative, hopeless, and frustrated thoughts were swirling through my head. I had already passed through the security gate at the base's main entrance and frankly, I do not know where the inclination came from, but I decided to pray to God personally, right then and there, as I drove. I had grown up with Protestant religious teachings and all, but I had never laid myself open, heart and soul and naked to God before as I did that day. I began to pray in desperation while driving. I said, "God, I am begging for your help. I don't know what to do. We are stuck here in a place that is not good for me and I can't think of anything more that I can do to make it better. We have no money or friends and my husband has no job. We have no one to turn to. I ask you to help me see a way to get through this. Please, I beg you!"

I am relaying my words as best I can. The thing I remembered most about that time was my sense of utter desperation. I let it go and left it to God.

Within a day or so, my entire attitude changed. I cannot remember any specific event or time that created the change in me. The realization that everything would be alright and that all I had to do was trust and keep on keeping on just came to me out of the blue. There was no actual "Aha!" moment. It was just there. I knew I just needed to do good works and hang in there and it would all be fine. I am sure I was taught this information in my sleep time; in the lessons and journeys we all make in our dreamtime as I had learned so many years ago from Edgar Cayce as a teenager in the library.

When I told Fran that God had answered my prayer, he said he could see an immediate change in me. I was calm and at peace. He said that from that moment on, I was changed. All I can say is, from that time I have been in love with God. All primitive fearful feelings I previously held about God and fear and judgment were swept away and I was left with a deep and abiding love for God. I came to know that the more I give to God, the more God gives back. God is infinite, as are God's blessings. I know that now. I did not know it then, but God chose to impart God's blessings and peace to a literal spiritual cripple, because that is what I was at the time. A few weeks later, Fran got a job and I started to make friends at my job. Some of these new friends were young Airmen, particularly females, who saw me as a fun, kind, mother figure who they could talk to. Some of them even called me "Ma."

When the bar was quiet, I would give them psychic readings. One of them told me that everything I ever told her came to pass in about three months. I was pleasantly surprised at the news; it showed I was developing a reliable ability.

I kept on with my studies and meditation unabated and I learned and retained…

Chapter 8
6th Decade

Nine Eleven came and went. I continued my bartender job as did the ghostly high-jinx at The Club. It seemed one of the ghost's favorite things to do to me personally, was to unlock a security door after I closed up for the night. On occasion, my supervisor would tell me when I showed up for work that the security police had found a door unlocked after I had closed up for the night. I apologized. It happened every now and then, with no regularity. I started doing two rounds of checks. A door was still, every now and then, found unlocked, usually at the Top Side bar. My supervisor started getting very annoyed at the unlocked doors, even threatening me with my job. Finally I said to him in desperation, "What do you want me to do? I can't fight a ghost and you *know* this place is haunted!" He would not argue or fire me because he knew I was not lying.

Besides The Club where I worked, there was also an Officers Club (The O-Club) a mile away. According to a fellow bartender, who was also an Airman, and who always worked the O-Club bar, it was haunted too. She told me the spirit person there would always hide things on her, only to be found later, somewhere else. Or things would disappear only to re-appear right back a few minutes later at the same place. Perhaps, another dead employee who chose to haunt for fun? That ghost exasperated that poor woman! Both of the described phenomena are a type of ghostly antics that are called apports.

In time, an evening came when the exasperated bartender was away on leave, so I got to take her shift at The O-Club for a change. My supervisor came up with a plan to meet me at The Club. Then, he would drive me to The

O-Club and pick me up at closing. He dropped me off near the front door, giving me a key and went to park the car in the back, as he had to bring in supplies on a hand truck through a back door. Upon opening the front door, I was greeted by a silent figure in the shape of a person made up of energy that looked like the "snow" on a television screen. I had prepared myself for anything there, so I just said to it, "Okay, I see you, but you can't scare me, so don't try any of your tricks with me because it won't work!" It immediately vanished. It never did make anything move or disappear on me and left me alone all night.

Another part of my job that night was to get prepared hot and cold food that my supervisor had left for me on tall carts from the kitchen that was down a hall at the building's other end. I then had to roll the carts with shelves of food on them up the long hall to the bar and set it all up on tables for the patrons when it was time for them to eat. Afterwards, I would return everything to the kitchen and leave the soiled food trays soaking in the sink for the kitchen staff to clean the following day.

The officers came in and I started to serve them drinks. It was the first time I had seen officers act like anyone else at a bar. That is, among other officers. I got the feeling that an officer's life can be a lonely one.

Eventually, the time came for me to get the food. Earlier, my supervisor had taken me down the long hall to the kitchen to show me where and what to do. At the time I felt a slight creepy feeling, but it was alright and it did not really bother me, as I had experienced spirit people before. But now, I was alone with no other living person's energy to distract me. I felt the uncomfortable feeling of being watched while walking down the hall. Upon opening the swinging doors to the kitchen, I felt a very heavy feeling indeed: someone was there who did not want me in *their* kitchen! In my mind's eye, I saw a middle-aged man in chef's clothes who was positively furious. I attempted to ignore him. I carefully slid the trays of food onto a rolling cart and brought it to the bar to set up. By now, the officers were merrily acting like any guys at any bar, and I drew comfort from their humanity and let the creepy feeling I had dissipate. The rest of my time working the bar went without incident that evening, and it was a pleasant job. Surprisingly, some of the guys even stayed and helped me to clean up. They were a real nice bunch of guys.

However, I dreaded having to return to the kitchen, but work is work, and it had to be completed, as I could not leave a mess. As I returned the dirty containers down the hall to the kitchen to soak, I felt the slow and steadily increasing creepy atmosphere of the hall again. Finally into the kitchen itself, the negative feeling seemed even stronger than earlier. I decided to attempt to find where he was by walking slowly around in a circle while looking out and psychically scanning the room around me. I came to an area where the feeling was strongest, and I realized I had "found" him. Instantaneously I felt that he was really, *really, pissed off* that I had. I turned quickly and finished my duties in the kitchen just as my supervisor arrived to pick me up. That was my first, and only, experience at The O-Club. Thank God, is all I can say. It was energetically draining to me.

Needless to say, I did not have much of a social life while living in the high plains. There are naturally occurring low areas where the water table shows in North Dakota that look like small lakes. These bodies of water were very popular with migratory and local birds of many different types. I spent many hours on the shores bird watching. That was my favorite part of North Dakota.

I also found great comfort in the Grand Forks Public Library. It was comfort, education, and solace. I began by studying autobiographical and biographical books beginning with the life of Ghandi. Next, I read every book they had about Edgar Cayce. Next, I graduated to borrowing as many audio books about spirituality and the paranormal that I could lay may hands on that interested me. I always went to where I was led as to choices of books or material. The more one allows this to happen, or even pretend, the more it will happen.

The land in eastern North Dakota is endlessly flat with roads running straight for miles that look like they are running into infinity. It got so I would drive for hours on end on the straight dirt roads of North Dakota while listening to audio books and not having to make a turn of the steering wheel or need to apply the brakes. On some of those drives, my consciousness would again go up and out of my head from time to time while driving due to the high frequency level of the information I was digesting in my mind. My body could still drive the car safely while my mind was above my head but still in the car below the roof. It was such a weird, amazing feeling I could actually feel my personal frequency rising while listening to the audio books.

Fran and I had a talk and we agreed to move back to New York. Eventually, I got a second job at a local convenience store to pay for our return to the east. I kept all my pay from that job in a separate bank account just for the move. About a third of the customers were local Native American people. As I did at every place of business wherever I worked, I called all the male customers Sir and the females Ma'am. To me, this is common courtesy. All people deserve love and respect, simply by the fact that they are living beings. At first, the Native American customers were stunned that I spoke to them thusly. Every human being wants and deserves respect and love! That's how I see it, at least. Long story short, because of the way I treated all the people, the sales went up because they came to where I worked for the pleasant experience. The Indian people were as nice to me as I was to them and when I walked along the road, they would toot their horns at me while waving and smiling at me and saying Hello. So unlike the local whites, who ignored me. To be honest, not all white people in North Dakota had closed minds and we did have a few friends there, but truth be told, we had more friends at the Grand Forks Air Force Base nearby where I worked, then in any town or city there that I experienced there.

Sad.

We moved back to New York state due to many reasons. I had a grandson who I had never met and for whom, my heart ached. I missed my family, especially my son. I missed my friends, especially, Pirate and MaryAnn. I missed the Hudson River Valley and its Highlands and the great varieties of birds and wildlife found there. I was sick of the flat lands. I was sick and tired especially, of nine long months of winter and having to shovel chest high snowdrifts. Not a good place for my spirit.

Adios, North Dakota.

So we moved back east to the humid land and settled into an apartment in Peekskill. I got a job right away as a bartender (again) and Fran found work through local contractors, which led to his job at the United States Military Academy at West Point. We re-connected with Chris and his family, as well as our own respective families. My grandson, Dylan, was now two and a half years old and cute as could be. We reconnected with old friends, like Pirate, and quickly made more new friends with the friendly New Yorkers. Life was good and my heart grew lighter; and I learned and retained…

Chapter 9

A Visionary?!

On March 20, 2003, the second Iraq War began. It seemed to me that the United States was always getting itself into yet another war. I guess the masters of war needed to fill their coffers with more blood money that flows like water during a war. I personally felt that President George W. Bush had a lame excuse for this latest, and to me, totally illegitimate war. What weapons of mass destruction? I was angry.

On a beautiful, sunny Monday morning on May 19th, ten weeks later, I went for a drive to enjoy the day. It was my day off and I was in a great mood. I ended up parking the car in the lot at China Pier on the Hudson River in Peekskill to relax and enjoy the view and the wonderful spring weather. I glanced at the time: it was 1 P.M.

I relaxed into a more comfortable, easy mood. I started to think about the war. I was very troubled within about it. How could such an awful thing be allowed to start to begin with? How could the supposed checks and balances of our government allow for such a waste of human life, not to mention money, by the president? It all made me sick at heart.

I then remembered Master Yogananda's words, "If you ask God honestly from your heart, he will answer you." I also remembered my experience of losing my car in Minnesota, when I asked God to help me, and I was helped immediately. I decided to ask God directly why this war had to be. By now, I had learned to trust God implicitly as God had also helped me in North Dakota when I asked for it. Besides, God had also given me an understanding heart when I asked for it as a teenager. (The big secret I learned is: you have to ASK FOR IT.)

While sitting in the driver's seat, I closed my eyes. I began to pray, asking God "Why and how could this bad war be allowed to be? I really need to know. Please. I need to understand the reason behind the war and all, so I can be happy and trust in You." I sat there with my eyes closed in internal silence. Not thinking, not waiting, just being.

I then began to feel my soul being gently lifted up, out of my body. I suppressed the instinct to open my eyes and allowed myself to go with the experience. To be honest, there is much I do not remember of the instruction that I received that afternoon. I remember being surrounded by white light. The next thing I knew, I was sort of flying/floating through space, but it was not the space known of by humans living on earth. It was all black, with no stars, but with a bright blackness that seemed limitless. It was *so* bright! All around me were, what I can only describe as celestial spheres. Each sphere was of a different color and size. Some had more than one color. All were absolutely beautiful in a totally non-three-dimensional way. Each more than a planet or solar system, more like a universe in itself, it seemed. Words are inadequate to describe them. I was in a state of wonder and joy. I was *so* happy! I looked around myself as I flew past and all around them. I heard a voice in my head, but from also up and above. It said, "All this is you, you are a part of all this. You are one with the all." The voice was neither male nor female, but neutral and gentle just like my voice I had heard all my life! I then realized that God was always there, all my life. Even in times of my childhood when I called myself an atheist! Later, after I thought about it, I came to the conclusion that God was probably real, so then I called myself an agnostic. Still, God and the voice were always there, regardless of my beliefs! I was filled with wonder, amazement, joy, humility, love, and total acceptance. God gave to me, and I gave back to God. Total love, total acceptance, moving both ways: me to God and God to me. I could not remember or think of any earthly love to ever match it. I was immensely happy. No, not happy; I was in exquisite joy, a state of bliss. I felt I was literally floating in a sea of total love. I had never experienced such a love before, and I knew I never would know such love on earth. I couldn't. This knowledge gave me no sadness, as I knew the bliss, such as I was experiencing at that moment, is impossible on earth. This is God's love, which is infinite. This is totally all right with me because to experience love like that will fill anyone with such total joy that you will never be the same again. It was as if there was only God and me, and that was more than enough.

I started praising God. "I love you, I love you!" I said again and again. I could feel tears of joy were falling from my eyes.

I began thanking God, saying, "Thank you, thank you for showing and teaching me all this. What can I do in my own small way with the small talents I have to bring this knowledge to mankind, so that they all will be comforted and learn the truth and be happy and know that we are all One with You and each other?

Immediately, all the spheres were gone, and I and I found myself floating in the empty bright blackness. I could still feel the love and comfort of God there, and I was unafraid.

The blackness disappeared to be replaced with a limitless whiteness. Suddenly, a black dot appeared ahead of me that spiraled outward, from the inner to the outer. Round and round it went, as words started to appear and spiraled out from the inside to the outside. Then the words ended, and symbols began to appear like flowers blooming in the center. It was immense, but I cannot tell you just how big it was in earthly terms. Was it two hundred feet across or two thousand miles? Earthly dimensions have no meaning where I was. "Get this out to the world, to teach them," the voice said. Since I was floating in space, I floated up and down and all round to study it. I just had to think of where I wanted to look, and I was immediately there, in an instant. It felt so natural and not at all strange, as a person on earth might imagine. I took a very long and careful time to study the symbol. I wanted to set it in my mind. I had to remember it correctly.

Then, very slowly and gently, I felt myself sinking back to earth, back into my earthly body. I could feel again the familiar heaviness of earthly three-dimensional energy. My eyes still remained closed. I still felt God with me, though I was back on earth. I continued to praise, thank, and love God, which I felt was reciprocated 100%.

I thought to myself, *Oh! If people could only know how much God loves them! Then they would never want to do anything bad to anyone because they would know that in attacking another, they attack themselves* and *God because they and others and God are all one. They would only be happy, love everyone, and know joy, as a child does.*

Would it make life on earth perfect? Of course not, but the knowledge changes people's attitudes and thereby their lives. They would innately know that all they really need is God, which is infinite, eternal love. They would lose needs that they cannot fill up, because they are no longer empty inside. They might even start to love everything they see, because what they see reflects themselves, as well as God. They would lose all their fears and internal emptiness and they would never want or need the ridiculous and unnecessary things of the earth. All blessings come from God. We just have to step aside and let God do it! We just need to get over ourselves and stop thinking we have to do anything, because God takes care of everything! This could indeed, be a heaven on earth if all mankind simply changed its collective mind.

I then felt God gently begin to move away from my space and allow me to become fully conscious. The first thing I was aware of, was that my head was bent back, like I was looking up at something. I raised my head and opened my eyes and became aware of tears all over my face and even on my shirt where it ran down because I had been crying tears of joy while unaware. Still, slowly coming back to "reality" I then checked my watch and discovered I had been "out and about" for three and a half hours! I had estimated 20 minutes at most! Fran would be home from work soon, so I headed home to start dinner.

Since that day, I have been forever changed. I would never view the world, mankind, and God the same way again. My heart is full of love for God and humanity and all that lives, for all are one to me now. I now see this world as the school of illusion that it is. I also know that no matter what happens, that it will always be all right. For me and everyone else, no exceptions, because that is how God loves us, with *no* exceptions. No one is higher or lower than anyone else, we are all one in God. Believe it or not, God is your best friend.

It took me two years to sketch and draw "The Key." That is my name for it. God did not give it a name, but I had to, because mankind needs labels for things, and I knew the symbol was the key to mankind's ascension. God did prompt me to have The Key copyrighted to keep it safe for good purposes only and not to be used for negative things. I did not know how to get it out to the world, but I trusted I would know when the time came. Then one day, years later, it came to me: I would write a book. So I got to work.

The Key

Part 2
YOU

Chapter 10
Welcome to Yourself

You are my friend. Odds are quite good I do not know you. But nevertheless, you are my dear friend. I cannot help but love you. You see, we are members of the same family. There is a little of you in me, and a little of me in you.

There is a little bit of everyone in everybody, everywhere. Our collective current understanding of DNA shows that. humanity is lusty and has spread its DNA to the far corners of the globe. Wherever people go, they procreate. There is a sizable portion of the present human race that has Neanderthal DNA, and to a lesser extent, Denosian, and then back to Homo Erectus. One Race: the human race. We may look different, but we are the same. We are one. You are one with everyone, me included.

Every schoolchild knows our bodies are composed of cells. Blood cells, nerve cells, bone cells, muscle cells, and on and on. Our DNA has triggers that shoot at the appropriate times during the development of a fetus so that what was once a zygote (a single cell of a combined sperm and egg), which divides and develops into what at first, looks like a primitive fish-like looking organism, and then eventually develops into what looks like a tiny miniature baby only inches long, which grows and develops until it can live on its own outside of the uterus and birth occurs.

Each cell of every body is composed of molecules, which are composed of atoms.

Atoms are composed of a nucleus and electrons. A nucleus is composed of protons and neutrons and is orbited by electrons. This is the same for stars, which are orbited by their respective planets. Each atom is like a miniature solar system in itself, spinning round and round. The rate of spin of the atom determines its frequency and atomic number. Another word for frequency is vibration. Everything has its own particular frequency according to its spin. The frequency is what makes a plant a plant, a rock a rock, or an animal an animal. The particular frequency of anything is the sum total of each individual atom's spinning along together with the frequency of the mind, which is separate from the physical brain.

Science has not, as yet, figured out how to measure this frequency and how to measure or manipulate it. Otherwise, many people on this planet would be able to change lead into gold. Science will eventually learn that it exists in a measurable way. We always had gravity before Newton figured out how to measure it; the same thing with x-rays, microwaves, and nuclear energy. It is just a matter of understanding and knowledge. Doctors used to practice bloodletting to rid the body of bad humors and believed that something invisible to the naked eye could not possibly make people sicken and die. Those practices and beliefs are now considered archaic. Science progress through slow, repeatable, provable study. It does not work by faith.

All the atoms of your body working together create your own personal frequency. The energy of your thoughts and actions add to it. Good deeds, gratitude, Love, and good thoughts raise your frequency. Bad deeds, as well as negative emotions, like hate, anger, and envy, lower your frequency. Of course, bad thoughts lower your frequency too.

Drop a pebble into a still pond. See the ripples spreading out? That is exactly how your very own thoughts and actions affect, touch, and move everything around you, including yourself. You see, your thoughts are actual *things*, not just nothing that touches nothing. If you think enough negative thoughts at a plant, for instance, it will fail to thrive, and it will literally die. So the same with people and animals being adversely affected by negative thoughts. Positive thoughts have positive effects. Dr. Masaru Emoto's work with water has proven that as scientific fact.

God created you not in physicality, but as a spirit, like God. In actuality, you were created initially as a wave of intelligent energy. God can create something only like itself, himself, herself; that is, as a spirit that is infinite and has the ability to create and is love personified. *that* is precisely what you are *right here and now!*

Our modern science believes that the physical evolved first and consciousness, second. That belief is erroneous. Everything is first created in consciousness (spirit) then second, into physicality. Physicality with no consciousness is not alive, but dead. From the inner (spirit) to the outer (physicality) is always how all life energy travels. This includes your personal life energy.

You are actually a spiritual being having a physical experience. When the physical body wears out, only the spirit remains. This is exactly what science has already proven: that energy is forever and it cannot be destroyed; it can only change frequency. Science however, still refuses to understand or accept just exactly what forever means in regards to the infinite energy that is your mind, as well as your own life energy. You see, when you die, your energy (soul) is forever. Death is an illusion. You will see your own body upon your own physical death. Your afterlife will be what you expect to experience. That is, what you believe in. Remember Peter Pan?

Besides being a spirit, like God, you also have the ability to create, as I mentioned before. People can obviously create by being artisans, architects, musicians, writers, et cetera, but you are also able to create your very world and universe by your belief in it from moment to moment. God thought, and the Big Bang happened. You thought, and your own personal universe was born. Your beliefs create your reality because as a child of God, *you* are the same as God with an infinite mind and power to create. A being who wants, and is, only love. The mind is the builder: as you sow, so shall you reap. So guard your thoughts, lest they come back and hurt you or the ones you love. *That* is the law of karma. It is not the next life, it is this one, here and now! Let no day pass that you do not speak a loving, kind word of cheer or encouragement to someone and you will find your own life uplifted, your own life opened, your love appreciated, and your purposes understood as well.

A life of good deeds and a spirit of gratitude will reward you here and now with amazingly good things coming into your now, blessed life. Every day is a chance to be happy. Every moment is a time to start. Do you want to be happy? Just *be* happy. Regardless. Nobody's life is perfect. Pass on the silly happiness to not only people you know, but to especially strangers. You never know what a smile or a kind word at the right moment may bring a miracle of help to someone and they might remember and bless you as some wonderful angel person who turned their life around in a moment. There is no human who will not respond in a positive way to loving kindness, because deep down, they subconsciously know they are worthy of it as a child of God, and they crave it subconsciously. Dare to be an angel to others. It's within you, I promise you.

You are living here and now to come to know who and what you really are. You have, no doubt, wondered what is the purpose of life. Why are you here? You are born, grow up, have a family, grow old, and die, to what purpose? Is it all for nothing? Are you just part of a bunch of little biological entities being born, lusting, reproducing, and dying? No, not for nothing: It's all for *you*, God's blessed child, so that you may awaken to who and what you really are!

You, yourself, set all this up prior to your present birth, on the other side (in heaven). You already knew everything before you came here. You were complete there. However, your job now here on earth is to remember here and now what you forgot from there and believe it here on earth and make it your own here and now. Thereby, you will be literally bringing heaven to earth and you will experience growth on a soulic level. That is, raising your personal frequency. Some people believe the earth is home. It is not. It is school, but like no earthly school. When school closes where do you go? You go home! Your true home is with God. That is, unity with God. You are part of God and God is part of you. You are part of the all. Never forget that.

There is a very good chance that the people that you know and love now in this world were part of your past lives. On the other hand, so are other people you have had bad experiences with. This is all set up by you and teachers who help you and wise ones on the other side so that you may come to know who and what you really are. That is, God's child. The wise ones I mentioned are ascended beings. They have evolved beyond the need for earthly incarnations and have chosen to be guides and teachers of a higher level. Sometimes, the wise ones decide to be born into the earth to bring teaching to humanity from the inner. Think of Jesus or Buddah.

God created you in His, Hers, Its image, That is, as a spirit, which is an intelligent energy wave with the power to create. What do you create? As I said, you literally have the power to create the world you live in.

You can change the circumstances in your life by changing you mind. Are things not going your way? Start the change by being appreciative of what you do have and like right now. Do not waste your energy thinking about things you do not like, as you will just bring more of those things to you. Be grateful every day for the good things in your life. I do not necessarily mean big things like a car for a house, though of course, it is important to be grateful for all things both large and small, but try at first to go small. For instance, did you wake up this morning? Many people do not. Can you take a walk down the street? There are many who cannot. Is there anyone or anything living in this world who loves you? A loving pet? Nice weather today? How about family, near or far, or the nice person down the street who is so pleasant that just looking at them makes you feel good inside?

How about being happy and grateful for something as simple as a good parking spot? Years ago I started the ball rolling for myself by saying out loud, "Thank you, God," for the first time when I found a perfect parking place for my car right where I needed to be. From that day on, it has snowballed and it is a very rare time that I do not get an excellent parking spot. Blessings magnified! The important thing is, do not take it for granted and stop being grateful, lest it go away. As it will. (But you can always get it back the same way.)

When you *totally* know you are truly one with God as well as everyone and everything else, you automatically know that you need nothing, because deep in your heart you are aware that you already have everything you need. That is, God and oneness. Not material things, they are nothing. They rot.

When you believe that you already have everything you need, because of acts of gratitude, you start to really see past the "hype" of this world and not need it. Do you *really* need the latest of *everything?* Perhaps your "mad money" would be better turned into deeds of loving kindness in donations to worthy people or causes.

Give it away – you will get it back magnified because you gave it away.

Do you really need that fur to keep you warm? Did not the animals who lost their own lives to make something for vanity's sake, not value their own lives as much as you value yours? Wool is warm and does not kill unnecessarily. Fashion is a lie that wants only to separate you from your money. So are cosmetics.

When you come to know and believe that since everything is truly energy, then you will come to understand that animals (who I like to think of as our little brothers) are energy, just as you and I are. Since energy is one, then you are also one with the animals, plants, and the earth, even the universe itself. Therefore, it is imperative you to treat everything with loving kindness, just as you do with people.

Animals have a heart, mind, and soul as you do. According to their frequency, of course. The plant kingdom has their own energy frequencies on a lower level than animals as well as a consciousness on their own vegetable level. Just think about it: all animals' bodies, from the lowest to the highest on an evolutionary scale, contain plant DNA. Did you know that plants know when you love them and thrive for you as a result of your loving them? We are all connected.

Modern physicists now talk of a "God Particle." However, it is not a particle, it is a frequency. You do not need a cell phone to transmit to someone, because all you need is your mind, which is energy. Again, this energy is presently unknown to science. Science still believes that the mind is in the brain, which it is not. The brain is a transducer of the mind, which is infinite and multi-dimensional. The mind is always connected to the other side, which is of a higher dimension/frequency than earths is. This is where your higher self resides while you simultaneously live your life on earth.

Simply thinking of someone alive or dead and you are instantaneously connected to them, believe it or not. Everyone, especially animals, are psychic. You just do not believe or know that you are. Animals can read your mind. They know your intentions for them. It is possible to learn to how to develop your psychic senses. It just takes sincere effort and some time.

Animals appear to be more psychic than people because they do not have belief "blinders" that people do, because people have freedom of choice, and animals do not. Man has learned how to tune out his higher self in his quest to be smart, sophisticated, rich, and modern. Animals live in the present and without judgment. They simply are. They simply are love. They simply are connected to the one in all, always.

Being psychic is as easy as thinking of someone and then they call you. That person's mind, which is energy, thought about you prior to calling you. You suddenly think about that person. Meanwhile that person is dialing your number. You may wonder how they are doing when suddenly, the phone rings. You answer the phone to find that very same person talking to you that you "just happened to think about" and you say, "Oh my goodness, I was just thinking about you…" That happened because their energy connected to your energy, and vice versa. You are "tuned into" that person as a radio tunes into a station's frequency.

The thoughts and actions of each living ling has its' own frequency and it is part of and parcel of the whole person, including the universe, both physically and spiritually. Therefore, if you want to be happy, then *be* happy. Emotion is a frequency you can tune into, either positive or negative. What your mind (you) pay attention to, you literally connect to that particular frequency of that particular thing, whether it be positive or negative. You become one with it.

What do you think of today's world or pop culture? Besides you having your own frequency, the entire world has its own which is a conglomeration of the mass mind all connected all the time and affecting (that is, creating) the world you live in en masse.

As said before, you have the power to literally create heaven on earth. It is like the story of Peter Pan: you just have to believe. How do you believe? By learning to see God (all that there is) in everyone. When you see everyone the same way, regardless of everyone's station in life, you will succeed, and you will experience great joy within because you will literally see nothing bad in this world. You will be seeing with the eyes of God. You must actually learn to love the unlovable. This is not easy, but it can be done with diligent attention to your thoughts minute to minute, with constant attention and correction. We are all a work in progress.

No one ever truly dies. How could they? They are part of the one, and since everything is part of the one, you are too. You will never be left out. Only you have the power to leave yourself out. Everything is energy/frequency and that energy is one (that is, connected) with everything, just as you are one with God. This energy moves continuously from the inner to the outer. That is, from God (spiritual/inner) to you (physical/outer).

This is why many ancient peoples created spiral designs. It represented the energy of the one in constant motion from the inner to the outer as below:

However, this drawing does not represent the infinite properly as it has an obvious beginning in the center. If the spiral is turned on its side and stretched out it looks different as in the second image:

Now to make it truly infinite, it would have to connect with no beginning and no end. Thusly, as represented in the third image:

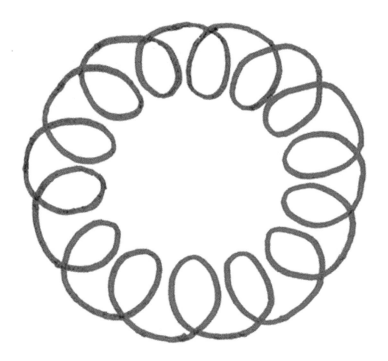

This image was shown to me in a vision while meditating for this book. I submit it for your consideration. Perhaps someone who has an open mind will get inspiration from it. I do not know if it resembles anything already in existence here on this planet at this time, but I would welcome any comments or information on this above image through the publisher.

Chapter 11
Heaven and Beyond

Heaven exists, but there is not just one. Just as God and the spirit of mankind are infinite, there are infinite heavens. Think of an onion, which has layers within layers.

Everything good in this world was first developed in heaven. Just as you were created on the inner within as spirit first, then became physical, later.

People living on the earth are continually inspired to invent, create and bring things from the inner to the outer as a means of development and progression.

When your physical life is over your spirit consciousness returns to the inner/other side/heaven. You may call it by whatever name you feel comfortable with, as there are no requirements, and requirement is an illusion, both on earth and especially, in heaven. For simplicity, I will refer to it as heaven here in this book, from now on.

At the moment of your physical death you will arise from the body you inhabited and lived in. You will see what people who have had near death experiences describe as a bright light. That is the light of God. You will, more than likely, then travel through a tunnel, which is actually a wormhole into another dimension: the dimension of heaven.

As you move along, the light up ahead grows brighter and brighter. Many people who have had near death experiences or NDEs describe the light they see as so bright that if they were looking at it with earthly eyes, they would be blinded, but their spiritual eyes see it just fine.

Some people, at the time of death, are afraid to go into the light because they believed what they had been taught about requirement, judgment, and damnation due to their supposed sins. They decide not to go on and stay where they are on earth. This is the most common way that people become ghosts. Another way that dead people stay and become earth-bound is that when they die they look down at themselves and see their astral body and think it is the physical body and stay on earth by choice. They think, *There's my inanimate body there, but I am here in a body, so I can't be dead.* So they hang around. Some people who die very quickly do not notice that they are dead and so stay on earth as a result. There are no requirements for anyone, living or dead. We always have free choice.

Edgar Cayce, the great American psychic, said that living people on earth are literally surrounded by thousands of ghost people all around them at all times. I believe him.

Some ghost people never leave the cemetery where their body has been buried; the cemeteries are full of ghosts. There are also ghost animals, but most ghosts are people.

Now, back to the tunnel. At the end there will be someone waiting for you to welcome you back home. Many times, it is a dead family member whom you love and trust completely. Sometimes, there is a loving, kindly elder/teacher to greet you. It is all a matter of your mental/spiritual level at your time of death, which determines who meets and greets you.

A child who dies gets the most gentle and kindly passage to heaven. Very often instead of a tunnel, children are gently led across a rainbow bridge by an obviously, wise, loving, and kind angel to a beautiful heaven awaiting them. If a child has already lost a parent or grandparent prior to their own passing there is a very good chance they will be greeted by that deceased person upon their arrival in heaven. Children are not afraid of death as adults are, as they have not yet lived long enough to learn to believe the earthly beliefs of necessity, sin, and judgment. They believe only in love, fun, and goodness, therefore, that is the only afterlife they will experience. Only children who have had their innocence taken from them will experience a different heaven, but one that heals and helps them completely.

Some people on their arrival see a river they literally float above and across to heaven. It all depends upon your personal beliefs, perceptions and level of development. Christians may see Jesus, Hindus Brahma, and Muslims Allah. Animists see their own vision of their own blessed one, and on and on. It is infinite and it is all for *you* with love.

Very soon after your arrival in heaven, you meet with a loving educator who shows you your entire life in an instant. You are then asked something like, "Do you feel you made good choices?" or "Do you think you did well?" then it is up to you. You will never be judged by another, regardless of what you had been told in your life on earth. You decide how you did. Perhaps you made what you think are negative choices. You then look within yourself and decide what you may have done differently. That is all. You may almost start to make a care plan for yourself for your future development. However, you are not required to do this at this point in time.

Since you are in heaven you, of course, get to have fun and enjoy yourself. You get to see and meet anyone you ever wanted to in life, in the past or even in the future because heaven has so time or distance. You can reconnect with animals as well, whom you knew and loved on earth. You can visit all the other heavens that exist, even the non-human ones. It is infinite, as are you. You can even take a trip home to visit earth or other planets as well-no space suit required.

There are conservatories of music in heaven that study, create and play all types of music, past, present, and future. There are grand concert halls that can literally stretch to hold an infinite number of attendees, even unto the millions or beyond. Earth is fixed in place, Heaven is not.

There are schools of art and architecture, past, present, and future. There are museums and infinite number for fun and study and laboratories of science and engineering that are developing future inventions and other developments for mankind. It is all part of things coming from the inner to the outer. That is, from heaven to earth.

Are you a foodie? Gourmet cooking and eating are alive and well in heaven, but nobody gets fat! (That's for *me!*) The greatest chefs of all time are happily busy in heaven.

All positive and creative pursuits are available to all who wish it. Whatever your joy and love, you may still enjoy, but on a grand scale and there is no need for money. Poverty does not exist. It all for free.

Heaven is like earth in that it contains plants and trees, land and buildings but not in a bland, earthly way. Buildings expand or contract to accommodate any number of persons. Their physical shapes would be impossible on earth.

The sky is not just blue as here on earth, but a soft, ever-changing swirl of colors with a soft sing song of different frequency sounds reflected there.

Plants glow from within with their aural energy force, and they can move and have amazingly beautiful flowers in colors and shapes that do not exist on earth.

Of the infinite number of heavens that exist, there are three that are set aside for different kinds of animals according to how they lived and moved about while living. One is of air for creatures that fly, such as birds and bats. Another is of water for creatures that lived in rivers, lakes, and the seas, and of course, one for land creatures. Each animal heaven is all perfectly perfect for each type of creature. Spirit people can go visit these heavens and re-connect with deceased pets and pets can visit spirit people when they wish too. Spirit people in heaven can visit great museums of learning with attached schools and workshops that show the history of all subjects past, present and future. These museums are also infinitely expandable as necessary to hold an infinite number of attendees.

There are actual after-world heavens that has its own respective shade of color that corresponds to the particular sort of people's mental inclination that inhabit it. As each color of the spectrum on earth has a different wavelength of the visible spectrum, so these places have their own color for the particular sort of mindset, course of study and interests that they collectively have. Each of them on first sight appears to be a city but it is much, much bigger: it is a universe unto itself. This is not in an astronomical third dimensional way, but in a celestial a higher dimensional way. They each appear to have a main dominant color, such as rose, yellow, green, blue, indigo, violet, and white. Each color represents a different area of study that is the energy frequency of each heaven's main area of interest. These include medicine, philosophy, science, the arts, writing, spirituality, and engineering.

One wonderful fact about death is that physical or mental limitations no longer exist in heaven. The blind can see, the deaf can hear, and the dumb can speak. All people who suffered with dementia or any mental disability are restored to their full awareness immediately. People either born deformed or injured while living are whole and beautifully normal again. Many people have actually chosen to be born deformed or to be injured at some point in their lives for lessons to be learned of a metaphysical nature for their own development and understanding. If the challenge is dealt with in a positive way, then the soul will grow in a positive way.

When the physical body is damaged on earth and loses a body part, the psychic anatomy still retains that missing member because it is spirit, not flesh. Someone born with a physical defect still has a perfect psychic anatomy that will be forever prefect and whole, despite earthly appearances. The reason for this is because the energy that is the psychic anatomy is forever whole and cannot be destroyed or damaged. People with a lost limb have phantom pain or feelings in it because it is still there energetically. You are forever, just not your body.

Eventually, all the fun, learning and study get to be enough and eventually you get to feeling like it is time to put into practice back on the earth school what you have learned in heaven. That is, to be reborn back into the world again in a new body. You see, your job is to come to know who and what you really are, but it is only when you put into practice on earth things you have learned in heaven and use it in a positive manner on earth, that true progression occurs.

To prepare to be reborn on earth an advanced teacher assists you to plan what you want to learn and accomplish when you return to earth in your next incarnation. To someone on earth it seems virtually impossible to arrange everything that comes with planning a new life for yourself. Just imagine: plans must be made for not only your immediate family and place of birth, but people that will come into your life both positive and negative, who will have an influence on your life. Also, places you go, schools you attend, work you do, how you die. You also choose alternative choices in your life because, of course, you will always

have free choice and you must have an almost limitless number of choices. It can be truly mind boggling, but somehow, it all gets sorted out. Before you are born you visit where you will live to familiarize yourself with your new home and family. You also set up your own future death, as strange as it may seem to you now.

When people have learned enough in heaven between lives, they will be ready to go back to earth and learn other things through trial and error again. In time people progress to the point where they do not need to reincarnate on the earth just to work on their karma anymore. Now life on earth is now a constructive choice.

Perhaps they may choose to come to the earth as a speaker. A speaker is one of the many souls who have chosen to come to earth to teach humankind the truth about themselves and God. There have been many speakers on earth.

Or, they can choose to learn how to use or manipulate energy in heaven. In heaven it is called energy work. You can learn how to literally create and control it and create your own little solar systems. This work is entirely yours alone to choose if you wish. There is a special place in heaven where these advanced students are taught advanced energy control. The students must learn to create conscious energy and make/help it grow into miniature solar systems and then mini universes that they tend to. Upon learning of this, I remembered there are two quotes about the subject "Ye may be as Gods" in the Bible. They are Psalms 82:6 and John 10:34. So never think lowly of yourself, because you are so much more that you can know or can imagine on earth.

One important last bit of information about heaven is that you and everyone else has, and always did have and always will have is their very own home G\group in heaven. These are spirit people with whom you have been together with as a group from the time of your creation to the now, all through your respective and collective "lives" as a part of the one. Kind of like a family, or a class in earthly school, but much more so. The term that I can best come up with to describe this is "Yours in God."

All home group members know each other intimately, and you will know your own that way. You all work together to help each other to learn and progress and to "become" endlessly, which is the most important part of your collective existence.

You also love each other limitlessly and would help each other at any time, whatever the reason, during or between lives. You all know each other intrinsically, more then you have ever known anyone in your earthly life. Not mother, spouse, or best friend on this world. That close. Does that frighten you, to be totally exposed? Be comforted, as God knows and loves you even better than that.

I awoke one morning with a definite memory that I had been in heaven visiting with my home group as I slept. I had been experiencing a very tumultuous time in my life then, and I was very conflicted. Apparently, I needed to talk and receive some guidance from the inner.

I remembered I seemed to be up in an atmosphere of some sort. The "sky" went infinitely both up and down and side to side. However, it was not blue as on earth. It was more like a multi-colored gently swirlies, like a soap bubble. The "ground" under my feet was a flat white surface, which appeared to have no discernable edges. It seemed that it could change size as needed. It was just suspended there in the atmosphere. Here and there, on the surface were geometric shapes for people to sit on, recline on, or lean against while standing and discussing things with each other. One of the shapes was an inverted half-globe, flat side up, just resting solidly on its curved bottom. People were sitting on, standing around or lying on the top of these shapes while conversing. Some of the taller ones were a bit high, but if someone wanted to sit or stand up there, they would just think about being there, and they were there immediately. They got down the same way, with no ungainly jumping up or down as on earth.

All the people wore comfortably loose clothing with very simple modest style that was totally lacking in ornamentation with no jewelry. All people had simple, natural hairstyles. It was obvious that this is a place that was specifically set aside for purely mental pursuits of a very loving all-inclusive nature. It was beautiful in a quiet, peaceful, non-ostentatious way. So *not* of this world!

One thing that I will never forget about was off to the side of this group area was a curved white stairway that went up to a small circular Greek-style temple. That small temple made a large, almost visceral impression on my mind. It gave me such a sense of familiarity and home. It seemed to me that it is a representative sign post of our home group's place and used for special occasions. I feel some sort of ceremonies were performed there. Also advanced souls use it as a conduit to visit and teach us as a group. I cannot specifically remember those occasions yet. I just have a feeling about it. I guess it is not something for me to have all the answers to, right now, and I can live with that. I choose to simply trust in God and know that all will be revealed when the time is right.

I knew it was important that I remembered my visit to my home group because I could then tell *you*, dear reader, the truth about yourself. The truth is, you are never forsaken by God. The only thing that can separate you from God is yourself and your beliefs. Your true home is not earth, it is not heaven, nor is it even with your home group in heaven. Your home is with God. It is only your erroneous personal belief of separation that keeps you separate from God. The truth is, you can *never* be separated from God, not even if you are an atheist and no matter what you may have done on earth. What sort of afterlife does an atheist get? Since you create your own universe by your belief in it, when your body dies and you believe that you will experience nothing, then that is what you will get: nothing. The poor soul is asleep, believing in nothing. However, God loves them, and they are not lost. There are nurseries for such souls, much like a nursery for newborn babies in hospitals. These sleeping souls are lovingly cared for by caretaker souls who have volunteered to care for them until they are ready to wake up to the reality of their permanence on a spiritual level. The caretakers gently probe the minds of the sleeping ones to help them to dream of their own permanence and to awaken naturally. Their sleep can last centuries, but all souls eventually wake up and realize who and what they truly are and get on with their personal business of progression.

Eventually, all spirit people (ghosts) hanging around on earth eventually will leave earth and move on. Everyone gets to go home to heaven.

Chapter 12
The Dark Side

As there are good and bad people living on Earth, so there are good and bad spirit people and entities as well. I would caution anyone to thinks that they can handle the dark side is mistaken. Even thinking about it (thoughts are things!) sends out an energy signal out like a lighthouse in all directions. This energy is touching everything and everyone, positive and negative entities, physical and not physical. This unwitting connection to negative energy will open you up to negative entities, who, will be drawn to you as a moth to a candle. Some would love to attack you and believe me, destroy you if given half a chance. I am talking about human spirits here, people who had lived and died. A person who had been a bad person in life is not suddenly going to be a kind and loving ghost. Until they actually move on to heaven and see who and what they are, they will stay mean and ignorant. Obviously, this kind of negative human entity is nothing compared to a non-human entity. That is, a demon. They are very rare and should be avoided at any cost. If you think you are being bothered by a demon, I would recommend the Roman Catholic church.

It is my sincere hope and prayer that reading this book will warn people off from attempting to play around with the dark side for fun and thrills. It is deadly serious, as I learned when a child from my nana and later, from personal experience.

God and the love of God are your best defenses against the dark side. Through personal experience I have found that when I get a dizzy feeling, nausea, or a pain, it could be an indication of a possible attack by an entity. However, it is also my personal experience that by thinking love at the entity, it usually stops them dead in their tracks if they are negative and they leave my presence right away. They love your fear as it is like a drug to them, and they want to mess with you. However, they run from your love. I have psychically heard entities screaming as if in pain when leaving my presence after I send them love and pray for them. It has never failed me. The effect is immediate and will only get rid of negative entities. I personally am just fine with the good ones around.

One proof the reality of the dark side is the Roman Catholic church and its practice of the Rite of Exorcism. The people who perform these rituals have studied and prepared themselves for many years to perform this service for mankind. It is psychically a very dangerous ritual to perform as they, in opposing the possessing dark entity or entities residing in a living human's body, may very well open themselves to attack. However, their training to become exorcists has prepared them to keep themselves safe from the dark side while freeing the possessed. These exorcists possess strong wills, faith, and minds to help them control their natural inclination to fear. Lately, the number of possessions and the need for exorcisms has increased tremendously as the dark side battles against the light, although they can never win and possess mankind. Humanity, despite the dark side's best efforts, *will* evolve and ascend soon. This will be a spiritual evolution and ascendancy, the age of aquarius, when the feminine water bearer pours out the blessings of God onto humankind. We just have to be ready for it and go with the flow.

I seriously warn against anyone who is not trained in the Ritual of Exorcism to not attempt to perform it. Ignorance will not protect anyone and will open you up to attacks and attachments. This also pertains to well-meaning people who attempt to clear a home of a haunting. What is shown in movies and television is entertainment, not instruction, and entertainment is not a substitution for many years of study.

What precisely do I mean by attack and how do dark entities attack? Practically everyone has seen on TV and videos the scratches and bruises that entities can leave on people's skin. This is nothing. They have many weapons to use against us. They can affect your emotions to make you angry, depressed, or even suicidal. Some want to break up marriages and families or even make a person kill members of their own families. They are capable of reaching into your body and damaging your internal organs to cause pain and even kill you.

They can suck away your life force making you progressively weaker till you die. People being attacked in this way will baffle medical doctors as medical testing often show nothing physically wrong. They are capable of pushing you downstairs, throwing projectiles, and causing things to fall onto living people. They can kill your pets. They can even enter an animal's body and make that animal attack you.

They particularly enjoy preying on children, as children are generally unaware of what is happening to them and they trust innocently. Children are naturally open to everything and negative entities often disguise themselves as spirit children and of course, children naturally want to play with a friendly child. Parents call them imaginary friends. They are not imaginary. This friend may turn out to be the opposite and turn your child's life into a living nightmare from which you have no physical way to protect them. To be in denial of such attacks can be extremely dangerous. It is very difficult, if not impossible, for the average person to fight an enemy that they cannot perceive with their own five earthy senses.

Popular culture has become almost obsessed with the idea of demonic entities and their attacks on people, but most of the negative entities who enjoy attacking people were actually human people once.

Imagine an insane person or serial killer preying on people in life. Do you think that upon death they will suddenly stop their mayhem? They continue it as long as they remain on the earth plane. They not only continue to attack living people, they even assault good human spirit people and control them like a kept herd of cattle. Only when the negative entity actually moves onto heaven will they receive the help and therapy they need and cure them of their nasty inclinations and to wake up to their own glory of the truth of the fact that they too, are God's blessed children.

However, dark entities can be demons, and not just negative spirit people. Demons are of course, associated with the devil, but demons can also be conjured (that is, created) by living people who dabble in the black arts or satanism. Since thoughts are things, it is actually possible for living people to conjure or create a demon. You just are not aware of the possibility. That does not mean that it is not true. That also goes for the fact that everyone is telepathic and psychic whether or not believe they are. So guard your thoughts carefully. Thoughts are *not* "nothing."

Living people also can create thought forms. Remember that your thoughts are real things, which can be either nice or nasty according to the frequency (nature of a particular thought, either positive or negative) that their minds create and send out, often unintentionally. Most people have no idea how many invisible weird thought form things are around that have been created by living people's minds.

So now, what can you do against this onslaught? There are methods of protection that you can use. One very good and simple method is to visualize your body (including your aura) surrounded by the white light of God's loving protection. Do this daily upon awakening for best results. You may visualize this any way you wish, just be sure you completely surround yourself. This method is also good to surround those you love as well, particularly the young, who do not have the mental capacity to do so. You can also use it to surround your home, friends, pets, or anything you wish to protect. The most important part is, that you must personally believe that it is protecting, and it will.

This is how I do it: upon arising, while getting dressed I see my entire self-surrounded by the while light of protection. I then set my intention that it will be there all day and all night. That is all that I need do.

You may also wish to add a prayer, or something else that corresponds with your particular beliefs. Just keep it positive.

Doing positive things to raise your personal frequency are also most beneficial. The higher your personal frequency is, the more you will automatically be protected from entities of a lower frequency, as they find it difficult to be in sync with your higher frequency. You can raise your frequency by being grateful and thanking God at least once a day for all the blessings and good things that come to you. Also, prayer will raise your frequency even higher, because you become in tune with what you pay attention to. So, the more you keep in touch with God, the more you will be protected, as God is the highest frequency there is.

Obviously, to be interested in dark subjects is not recommended, so try to stay in the light and remain positive in thought, word and deed. Please, my dear one, for your own good do not attempt to join groups that are into satanism, or any likewise organization. It will hurt you on a spiritual and soulic level, the like of which you cannot imagine. You will open yourself up to negative attachments at the very least. I cannot stress this enough! If you ever sense that a negative entity is bothering/attacking/near/scaring you, immediately order it forcefully, "In God's name, be gone evil one!" Then change any negative habits you may have acquired and stay in the light. Surround yourself with God's white light of love and protection. Then trust and know in your heart that God is watching over you.

I have learned that paranormal pursuits such as scrying, divination and even casting spells can be safe to perform as long as a prayer of protection is always used prior to these efforts, and that it is used only for positive endeavors.

Do not hold grudges or be unforgiving of anyone because that negative thought energy will come back and bite you in your behind as quick as karma. Instead, forgive others and forgive yourself, for finding fault in others. This, by the way, is a personal healing for you on a divine level. You see, when you forgive and love others, especially those who are injurious to you, you are literally seeing them through the eyes of God and behaving just like God, again raising your personal frequency level even higher. God *never* judges anyone or sends people into damnation, regardless of the erroneous information you have been taught in the past. We damn ourselves.

Unresolved hate and judgment not only lowers your frequency, but can also affect your body on a molecular level and make you ill and even give you cancer. Change your mind and change your life, as well as your frequency.

Ghost hunts and investigations are not recommended except by and with reputable investigators. Empty, old, run-down buildings can be dangerous on both a physical and paranormal level. Trespassing to find ghosts can land you in jail. Even nice entities can get riled up if not treated with respect, love and understanding. All persons, living or dead, can get annoyed or even angry when mistreated, let alone, negative entities, and not many living people can tell whether people are good or bad, especially if you cannot see them. So be careful. This is serious shit.

It is for your own personal good that you take responsibility for, and care of, your own spiritual progress. Although there are no requirements, why waste your own time on earth being fooled by the illusions of this world?

You have the power to create a heaven on earth as you are meant to do. You have the power to do it with your mind by acting as if, and living as if, it already is.

Then you can grow and learn in the here and now on earth and come closer to God. You will actually come to know that you can make a heaven on earth because that is only what you see and believe in, not this world of illusion. Peace will come to the earth when a generation is born who loves peace above all else. Death is an illusion as you are forever, and you create this world as it is by your belief in it just as it is now from moment to moment. Change your mind and change the world you see. It is possible to see every person as God's blessed child. God gave you the power. Remember, and use it, but for good, as God does. God made and created you. God is incapable of making anything bad. You are *not* bad, no matter what you have done in an earthly way. Therefore, forgive yourself and others as God already does, and go and sin no more. The truth *will* set you free, but you have to choose it freely. Choose to be what you truly are: a loving child of God. In truth, you cannot be anything else. Everything else is an illusion. You have *no* idea how much God loves you! If you felt, for only a second, God's love that I felt the day I received The Key, you would never want to separate yourself from God ever again, because the bliss would be so exquisite, you could not bear to do what is not good, because it would separate you from God's love which is always yours freely and eternally for the taking.

Why would you ever separate yourself? Do you believe deep down that you are unworthy? Oh no, you are never unworthy of God, no matter what you may have done. Even someone who is a thief, a murderer, a torturer is still and always God's beloved child, and is worthy of so much more then so many people have decided upon for themselves by self-condemnation. God is actually part of you just as you are *right now!* God created you so that through your experience, through which, God also experiences, so that God may also come to know God as Himself, Herself, Itself, just as you need and want to know (understand) who and what you are as well! So do not be afraid of God. God loves you just as you are. Forgive yourself, just as you are, and ask God with a sincere heart to come into your life *now* and God will hear and help you.

When you get to psychically hear God you will hear the voice in your right ear only. The negative can only come through your left side. God is always on your right. (As an interesting aside, that is why adults used to train left-handed children to do things, such as writing, with their right hands instead.)

Things of God make you happy and joyous. Things not of God create fear and separation. Follow your heart and know that your heart is where God dwells.

The more you come to truly know and understand that the three-dimensional world of illusions and requirement is just an energy wave and that it is entirely your choice as to whether or not you react to, or be a slave to, this world of illusion. It appears as if it is becoming increasingly more negative. Actually, the opposite is happening, but the negative side will fight to the very end as long as it can, to ensnare as many human souls as possible before the actual ascension is complete.

Do not be fooled by the naysayers. The positive change has already begun, I promise you, from the bottom of my heart and soul.

Spiritual growth demands a temporary surrender of security. It is not easy. However, you by your own choice came here to the earth by choice again to learn who, and what, you really are. In truth, you are not a physical person with a head, body, extremities, and a pee-pee! Instead, you are a wave of intelligent, multi-dimensional energy, which is forever and cannot be destroyed, ever. Your personal energy frequency can only move up or down. Even our science, such as it is, has proven that energy is indeed, forever.

It is not easy to truly understand that everything you believe you see is not real. It is no more solid than air, which you walk through. You must learn to literally see this three-dimensional world for the illusion it is. Then, you can learn to have fun with the illusion and make your world how you want it to be for you! Instead of being a victim of the world, you can have a life of eternal internal peace and unending happiness. Change your mind and change your world! Change your mind and start being grateful to God for even the small things you have. For instance: the birds are singing, the sun came up to warm your face. So simple and yet, when you actually do it from a sincere heart, you will see how good things will just multiply in your life. Just like mini miracles that happen and make you happy and grateful! It may sound contrary, but you will be amazed at how blessings literally fall into your lap in time. Just develop the habit and do it whenever you think of it, as often as you like. Regardless of, and when bad things happen, because they will, as you are currently living on the imperfect earth. Forgive those negative things and let go of them and cling to the loving kindness that lives within you.

One mantra (a short, repetitive prayer) that I came up with that has helped me to see the illusion of this world is "Take me to truth." I would repeat it aloud whenever I thought of it. Very shortly, my time of meditation and introspection opened me up to more knowledge and happiness. I came to understand and know that I am part of the one. That is you, me, all that has ever lived or will ever live, as well as God are all part of a vast oneness that is immeasurable, infinite love. There is literally no beginning and no ending, just the eternal love and time of God's *now*.

When you are troubled, pray for guidance. God already knows exactly what your problems are and what you need. Do it intimately, without judgment at all and God will hear, but you have to *ask for it* yourself. There is nothing special to say, just what is in your open heart. Ask just once. Then wait and trust the answer that comes from within and go with it, whole-heartedly, especially if the answer feels good and safe inside you and gives you peace or happiness. God will never scare you.

Nothing that comes from God will be bad. It can bring you peace, joy, inspiration and all sorts of good things, but it will never feel bad to you inside, or give you a bad feeling, or tell you to hurt yourself or others. Those, and all other bad feelings are not of God and must be told to go away immediately and then ignored.

Since you are energy, the energy of the things you pay attention to will affect you either positively or negatively according to their own frequency. Your energy can, and will, become "in phase" (matching frequencies) with earthly things that you surround your life with, whether they be good or bad.

For instance, what kind of music do you listen to? What movies, games, TV shows, websites, books, videos, and pastimes do you fill your life and mind with? What sort of people do you have as friends? Are they kind and supportive people, or not? As I said before, you become in-phase (frequencies aligning to match) with what you pay attention to and it is easy to fall into the pit of the popular culture of this time. Nobody wants to be an outsider, do they? But, is your life serving you, or are you serving it? Perhaps your phone is taking you away from listening within and looking for the positive way to go, rather than run with the negative. You are in charge and you have the choice, always.

By patient study, prayer, meditation, and introspection, you can help yourself along the way. We are all blessed in the present to have free access to the internet. What took me decades to find can now be found in minutes. Unlimited websites, information, not to mention, opinions, are available at a keystroke. So, where do you start? Try to trust your internal instincts and go where you are led and go with that and let it be. Are there any subjects that excite you or have been very interested in, perhaps for years? That is a good indicator of where to start. You see, the more you learn to trust this process, the easier and more automatic it will get. Just be sure that what you study is positive, not negative. If you wish, ask God to lead you in the right direction, and trust in the good things that you will find.

A good place to start is to learn about the world's different religions. What are their basic doctrines? Do some resonate more with you than others? How are they different or similar? Do you like some parts of some religions and not other parts of them?

Other possible areas of study are ancient mysteries, philosophy, archeology, the occult and metaphysics. Other good places to search are the world's worlds various native cultures' mystical beliefs and ancient history. This is a miniscule list, as there is a veritable plethora of information out there. Sometimes children's books with their simplicity are a good start.

I would also urge you to check out your local free library before looking anywhere else. Simply start at the beginning of the non-fiction section. That is where the paranormal books are kept in all libraries. You may find it easier to simply pull a book off the shelf and let your eyes scan it quickly to help you decide what you really want to invest the time and then put it back, if you wish, with no commitment, rather than having to deal with the hassle of returning a book you had decided against that you had ordered online through the mail.

Always listen within when choosing books or subjects of study and learn to trust the positive promptings that you get. If the prompting you get comes from within you and it does not scare you, and it gives you a feeling of joy or a good/happy quickening within you, than follow your instincts. The more you actually *use* this way of scanning books (not to mention anything else in life) it will get easier for you.

In time, you will soon learn to trust those feelings and act on them, for a positive outcome and life.

The more you learn about paranormal inter-dimensional subjects, the more you will eventually realize that everything you are learning is actually something you already knew deep inside on a soulic level before you even learned it in the now.

How can this be? Because you need to bring everything you already know from the inner (heaven) to the outer (earth) and live it here on earth and believe it and make it your own so that you will progress to a higher level.

The fact is this: You are created of God and you are God's perfect child. You are God's beloved one, just as you are. Right here and now, warts and all. God is love and you are love. God can only act and create in love. God gave you free choice since God wants you to know who and what you are, freely. (Animals do not have free choice; they just are and accept life as it is.) When at last, you are ready, you will come to an implicit understanding of the facts of exactly who, and what, you are and you will begin to be happy in a heavenly way. As you live your life and give away love to everyone and everything you meet, your happiness will grow into joy. You will in time, become aware of the truth and you will come to know who and what you are in an even more expanded way. To God you are perfect and blessed and loved perfectly, just as you are. You do not have to lose those extra pounds. You do not have to have the right religion. You don't have to look good. Or be smart. You do not have to be straight or normal. You do not have to be dressed right or have the latest thing. You do not have to be beautiful or young or popular or especially rich and famous.

Now, don't you feel better? Whew! All the pressure is off and now you can relax and enjoy life. Now you can have a life filled with joy. That is, if you believe you deserve it.

A life filled with joy does take a bit of work. You have to work at being loving and kind to other forms of life, especially people. All people. Again, there are no requirements and you can live a miserable life if you so choose, but why do that?

That is just plain silly, at the least. Also, you may decide to work at developing a sense of gratitude to God who freely gives blessings into your life if you only choose to become aware of them. The best things in life are not things. Love is the best thing, especially, spiritual love. Next best is familiar love like family members, or other people, like friends, that you love. However, physical love does not last, it cannot. It is physical. Nothing physical is forever. Only spiritual love is forever, as are you forever, as is God.

Take time for your quiet times alone to go within yourself. Use introspection to look at the many choices you make daily. Were they positive or negative? How could you have improved any choices you made? Did you experience any negative reactions to people, memories, or things? Then make changes in yourself, if you feel you need to, but lovingly, without judgment just as God looks at you without judgment and with only love. Like God, you and I are in a constant state of becoming. We have been given free choice as to what and who we become.

Why would you attempt to bother to be negative rather than positive since God loves you so and has no requirements of you? This world is simply a school, and you know how school is: it closes and then you go home, and now you know where Home is, because I told you.

Nothing is ever easy. It is not supposed to be that way. Otherwise we would learn nothing from our earthly experiences. However, become aware and nothing is ever really hard again.

The care and tending of your mind and soul is one of the most important aspects of your life here, if not the most important, and is exactly why you chose to be incarnated into the world at this time for your greatest good, believe it or not. The negative things in life that befall us all are things you and I had picked ourselves for our own personal challenges in our current life prior to our birth on earth. The saying, "God never gives us more than we can handle," is true as we have chosen our challenges when we are in our higher selves when we are in heaven. If you choose to hang in and do not give up, or succumb to temptation, or pass a negative judgment on the challenge, you will be richly rewarded by heaven *here and now* in this life and you will see how you are progressively becoming a better person because of having turned a negative into a positive. You will experience redemption on a personal level.

I have had personal experience with this concept. When a pre-teen, my grandson came down with a childhood cancer. The entire family was devastated, myself included. However, I already understood about negative experiences in life as being an opportunity for personal growth and I tried very hard not to allow myself to become despondent. Many times, I prayed to God to "help me see the blessing in all this" as I cried.

It did not happen overnight, but over the months, then years, I became involved with on-line prayer groups and I began to send loving, healing thoughts to Dylan and sent him emails giving him encouragement. When the day came that I knew he was going to be cancer-free eventually, I told him so.

I also made a determined effort to get over my feelings of personal loss due to Chris and his family moving from New York to North Carolina years previously. I kept on pushing myself to be in a mental state of positivity regarding the entire matter. Bit by bit, a change did come over me and I felt better not only about my grandson's health, but basically everything else too. Guess what? As of this writing, of May 2020, Dylan has been cancer-free for seven years, and I am comfortable with where they live and I love them all happily and life is good. How silly of me to limit love! It is amazingly easy to get caught up in the illusion that love can be limited by time or space. Although I have been studying metaphysics for more than fifty years, and people may see me as a soothsayer or a wise woman or whatever, but I still am fooled by the illusions of this world to a greater or lesser extent on a daily basis. I try to stay aware of this consistently, so I can return my mind to a positive and forgiving aspect without self-judgment to myself, or others. As I have been saying for many years, "pobody's nerfect."

You and I are collectively working on our spiritual growth, whether or not you remember that you are. We are working together collectively for freedom from illusions, the three-dimensional world, and belief in requirements. We all have an in-born desire to be totally aware of truth.

Introspection and self-understanding are very important methods for your personal progress. Ask yourself, why do you react to, or feel the way you do to some people and not so to others? Is there anyone that you can remember, that when you first met them, for some reason you immediately did not like that person? Or, on the other hand, did you ever meet someone you immediately liked, and felt drawn to? Both positive and negative feelings are good indicators of people from past incarnations' worldly experiences as well as time spent together in our true life between physical lives. We meet, not by chance, those with whom we had set up a date with, in heaven prior to our birth here on earth to get together at the appointed time and work on issues that remain from previous lives that come up again in this, your present life.

How do you feel about other nations, other races, countries, or different historical periods in time?

Ask yourself quietly within, "Why do I feel this way about so-and-so?" just once and let it go. You may see a sudden picture flash in your mind that immediately goes away. Or, you may get a sudden feeling in the pit of your stomach, like when you meet or think of someone from your past that does not feel good to you. Rather than ignore that feeling or try to mentally push it away, instead, mentally lean into the feeling and look at it. As they say, "What you resist, persists. What you look at, goes away." Perhaps you may see an image, get a feeling or get a knowing within. These are valid clues and can be keys to self-understanding and getting in touch with your true multidimensional self. This may not happen the first time you attempt this but keep at it. Your psychic senses need to be exercised to get strong too, like your physical muscles. Mostly, the things you will sense are things that are energetically and emotionally charged. This can often happen when you meet someone new, or when a change in your life occurs.

Change is part of life this three-dimensional world and is necessary. Without change, all things rot and die on earth. Sometimes change will appear to be negative or even destructive in a physical way, but the change will always prove to be positive in the end. As the Siene wave goes up and down, so do you and your imaginary lives. It is imaginary because you are actually one with God, and *are* with God, rather than living the life you now think/believe you are living. You just do not believe you are deserving of that wonderfulness right now because you believe you're just "Little-old-me" but you are already *right there* in the bosom of God! You always were, even if you do not believe in God, because God believes in you and loves you infinitely, regardless.

The secret is to see the positive in the negative, which is an illusion anyway.

Always try to do the right thing at all times and try to put others first before yourself. Remember, in the end, it is only all about you and God, nothing else. Truly, you do not have to do anything, all you have to do is *be*...and listen within, which will lead you down a path of righteousness and joy. There is an excellent chance you will be amazed and smile at the blessings that will freely come your way if you do. There is also an excellent chance that you may be tempted to kick yourself in the seat of your pants for not realizing this sooner.

Part III
GOD

Chapter 14
What God Is Not

God is not angry, needy, or judgmental.

God will not send you to hell, no matter what. You can send yourself to hell by your beliefs. Hell is a state of mind in another dimension. Hell exists because people believe in it.

God does not hate, regardless of what other people may tell you. They are in error, those who tell you such things.

God will never see you as unworthy, even though you may believe that you are, which is another error. Your belief creates your illusion of unworthiness.

God does not care or notice how many errors you make. God sees you as you are: God's blessed creation.

God is not silly enough to be jealous because: God is *all there is*. That means God has no requirements. How could He/She/It?

Therefore, the day will come in your own personal spiritual evolution when you come to realize that you were, and are and will be, just like God already from the day of your creation by God.

When that blessed day comes, you will lose your negative beliefs and emotions because you will not need them, and you will be just as God is: all loving and seeing the one in all, and your horizons will become endless, as are God's.

Chapter 15
What God Is

All that is – is God. That includes not only yourself and other people, but also what are considered bad people/things too, as well as everything you can see and everything you cannot see.

> God sees all people equally and blesses all people equally, regardless.
>
> God always sees you as you truly are – His/Her/Its beloved one, regardless of how low or unworthy you may believe you are.
>
> God, like you, is in a constant state of becoming. God created you so that through your experiences, God may come to know God better.
>
> God never stops "Godding."

Regardless of what you have been told, God does *not* condemn or judge, nor does God require anything from you. That said; God would *love* to have your love! Perhaps, therefore, we should not judge others? What do you think? Huh?

Only you can separate yourself from the love of God, but God always loves you anyway because God cannot separate from you because you are God's child.

God loves unconditionally and infinitely.

If you feel you need to ask God to forgive you for something you have done, then do so, as it will help you to forgive yourself, which is something you will ultimately do in time. When you forgive yourself and others as well, you automatically become in sync with God. This is because God knows there is nothing to forgive in you. You have to come to the point of complete forgiveness and then change your ways. Then you will remain, always, as you were created: a blessed part of God. Forever a perfectly loved, esteemed part of all-that-there-is: which is God. All-that-there-is includes you too, you know. Do you know what this means? This means that you are not only a being that is a part of God. It means that you are *just like God.*

Therefore, you are *one*, you are love, you are good, you are eternal, you are multi-dimensional, you have the power of creation, and *you are that you are!*

Just Like God!

Books/Bibliography

Most of these books are in my current library. I have easily read four times as many. I have also given away innumerable books to help others on their own paths. Some I could never forget and thusly, am able to recommend them. In many cases authors have written more books than I have recommended, but I only list books I have personally come into contact with. I am sure I have forgotten many. If you feel drawn to any specific ones, I recommend you start with those and see where your own path leads you. May you find joy on your own voyage of discovery!

Namaste. (That means the divine in me recognizes and honors the divine in you.)

In Love & Light,
Linda

In alphabetical order by author:

Albom, Mitch: *The Five People You Meet in Heaven*
Alexander, Eben M.D.: *Proof of Heaven*
Aligeri, Dante: *The Divine Comedy*
Altman, Nathaniel: *The Palmistry Workbook* *
Alvarez, Melissa: *365 Ways to Raise Your Frequency*
Andrews, Ted: *How to Uncover Your Past Lives*

Bergen, Jacqueline Syru & Sr. Marie Sekwan: *Forgiveness a Guide for Prayer*
Bernstein, Moray: *The Search For Bridey Murphy*
The Bible
Birkbeck, Lynn: *Do It Yourself Astrology* *
Blavatsky, H. P.: *The Secret Doctrine*
Bodine, Echo: *Look for God and You'll Find God*
Brown, Michael H.: *What You Take to Heaven*
Brown, Rosemary: *Unfinished Symphonies: Voices from the Beyond*
Buckland, Raymond: *Practical Candleburning Rituals*
Campos, Sydney: *The Empath Experience*
Cayce, Edgar: *A Search for God, Books 1 & 2 The Power of Your Mind Reincarnation and Karma*
Christy, Lynn Sparrow: *Beyond Soul Growth Awakening to the Call of Cosmic Evolution*
Coelho, Paulo: *The Alchemist*
Cohen, Alan: *Dare to Be Yourself*
Crowley, Aleiister, edited by Symonds, John & Grant, Kenneth: *The Confessions of Aleister Crowley*
D'Alvia-La tourrette, Br. Victor-Antoine: *Walk in His Ways*
Denning, Melita & Phillips, Osborne: *Practical Guide to Psychic Powers Awaken Your Sixth Sense*
De Saint-Expuery, Antoine: *The Little Prince*
Deveaux: Paul: *Earth Lights Revelation*
Decoz, Hans & Monte, Tom: *Numerology Key to Your Inner Self* *
DeSaint-Exupe'ry, Antoine: *The Little Prince*
Dillard, Sherrie: *Discover Your Psychic Type*
Dixon, Jeane: *My Life and Prophecies*
Doochin, Lawrence: *I Am Therefore I Am Revelations of Truth*
Edward, John: *One Last Time What If God Were the Sun?*
Foundation for Inner Peace: *The Course in Miracles*
Fox, Matthew: *Illuminations of Hildegard of Bingen*
Frissell, Bob: *Nothing in This Book Is True, But It's Exactly How Things Are*

You Are a Spiritual Being Having a Physical Experience
Fuller, John G.: *The Interrupted Journey*
Gabran, Kahil: *The Prophet*
Gach, Gary: *The Complete Idiot's Guide o Buddhism*
Greenaway, Leanna:
Hahn, Thich Nhat: *Creating True Peace*
Hawkins, David M.D.: *Power vs. Force*
Hesse, Herman: *Siddharthra*
Hicks, Robert: *Living Simply in an Anxious World*
Hoffman, Enid: *Develop Your Psychic Skills*
Karcher, Stephen: *How to Use The I Ching*
Klauser, Henriette Anne: *Write It Down, Make It Happen*
Kuthumi & Dwal Kul: *The Human Aura How to Activate and Energize Your Aura and Chakras*
Lang, Ade'le & Rajah, Susi: *How to Spot a Bastard by His Sun Sign*
LaVey, Anton Szandor: *The Satanic Bible*
Mack, John E M.D.: *Abduction Passport to The Cosmos: Human Transformation and Alien Encounters*
MacLeod, Ainslie: *The Instruction: Living the Life Your Soul Intended*
Margolis, Char: *Questions from Earth, Answers From Heaven*
McTaggart, Lynne: *The Field*
Milton, John: *Paradise Lost*
Montgomery, Ruth: *Aliens Among Us Companions Along the Way Here and Hereafter A Gift of Prophecy:*
The Phenomenal Jeane Dixon: Herald of the New Age
A World Beyond: A Startling Message from The Eminent Psychic Arthur Ford from Beyond the Grace
The World Before
Moody, Raymond, PHD, M.D.: *Life After Life Reunions*
Muhammed The Prophet: *The Quran*
Newton, Michael PhD: *Journey of Souls Destiny of Souls*
Norman, Ernest L: *A Beginners' Guide to Progressive Evolution Cosmic Con-*

tinueum
Elysium: The Pulse of Creation Series
The Infinite Concept of Cosmic Creation
The Infinite Contact
Infinite Perspectus
The Truth About Mars
The Voice of Eros
The Voice of Hermes
The Voice of Muse
The Voice of Orion
The Voice of Venus

Norman, Ruth E.: *Biography of An Archangel-Accomplishments of Uriel*
Bridge to Heaven: the Return to Atlantis Ra-Mu of Lemuria Speaks
Return of Atlantis
Tesla Speaks Series

Prahuboda, A. K. Bhaktivedanta, Swami: *The Bhagavad Gita As It Is*
Krishna The Supreme Personality of Godhead The Science of Self-Realization

Panker, Derek & Julia: *The Comlpeat Astrologer's Sun-Sign Guide*
Pelican, Jaroslav, Editor: *The World Treasury of Modern Religious Thought*
Pepin, Eric J.: *The Handbook of the Navigator*
Rampa, Lobsang: *You Forever*
Redfield, James: *The Celestine Prophecy*
The Celestine Vision

Reed, Henry: *Your Mind*
Renard, Gary, R.: *The Disappearance of the Universe*
Rinpoche, Padmasambhava, Guru: *The Tibetan Book of the Dead*
Roberts, Henry, C : *The Complete Prophecies of Nostradamus*
Roberts, Jane: *The Seth Material*
Seth Speaks
The Education of Oversoul #7 (From the Oversoul Trilogy)
The Nature of Personal Reality

Rufus, Aneli: *Party of One the Loner's Manifesto*
Sanchez, Nouk & Vieira, Tomas: *Take Me to Truth Undoing the Ego*
Sendak: Maurice: *Where the Wild Things Are*
Sorrell, Roderick & Amy Max: *The I Ching Made Easy* *
Stern, Jess: *Edgar Cayce, The Sleeping Prophet Immortality*
    Intimates Through Time: The Life Story of Edgar Cayce and His Companions Through the Ages
    The Search for A Soul Taylor Caldwell's Psychic Lives
Sutphen, Dick: *You Were Born Again to Be Together*
Van Auken, John: *Edgar Cayce On the Spiritual Forces within You From Karma to Grace*
Von Daniken, Erich: *The Chariots of the Gods*
Vost, Kevin Psy. D: *Unearthing Your Ten Talents*
Walsh, Neale Donald: *Communion with God Conversations with God*
The New Revelations A Conversation with God Tomorrow's God
Weiss, Brian L, M.D.: *Same Soul, Many Bodies*
Woolfolk, Joanna Martine: *The Only Astrology Book You Will Ever Need*
Zolar: *Encyclopedia of Ancient and Forbidden Knowledge*
Zukav, Gary: *Seat of the Soul*

    *These books were part of my curriculum from correspondence course.

Recommended People/Places/Sources/Things of Interest
(Besides, obviously, the authors of all the above books)

abebooks.com
The Association for Research and Enlightenment, Inc. (The A.R.E.)
Babaji
Bear and Company
Bruno, Giordano
Cayce Quarterly Magazine (A.R.E. Membership benefit) edgarcayce.org
Chautauqua Institute, New York
Coleman, Loren
The Crystal Connection, Wurtsboro, New York
The Dalai Lama
Douglass, Fredrick
edgarcayce.org
Emoto, Masaru, Dr.
Fate Magazine fate.com
Fatima, Portugal: Marian Sightings
Fox Sisters, The
Franklin, Benjamin
Garabandal Spain: Marian Sightings
Ghandi, Mohandas
Holtzer, Hans & Erika
Hopkins, Bud
iamthereforeiam.com
I – Ching

Icke, David
Infinitewaters (Diving Deep)
Jesus of Nazareth
Jung, Carl
Karma Cards by Monte Farber
Keller, Helen
King Jr., Rev. Dr. Martin Luther
Leek, Sibyl
Lighthouse Curiosity Shoppe, Sugarloaf, New York
Lily Dale, New York
Lincoln, Abraham
Llewellen Worldwide
Lourdes, France: Marian Sightings
Queen Christina of Sweden
Roosevelt, Eleanor
The Rosecrucians
Sedona, Arizona
Self-Realization Fellowship Magazine available from: yogananda.org
Smart, Ralph
Summit University
Swedenborg, Emmanuel
Theresa of Calcutta, Saint
Tesla, Nikola
Tubman, Harriet
unarius.org
Venture Inward Magazine (A.R.E. Membership benefit) edgarcayce.org
Warren, Ed & Lorraine
worldprayergroup.org
X, Malcolm
yogananda.org
Zoroaster